W9-BHE-939

HOUSEWARMING

PROBABLY THIS

HOUSEWARMING

A GUIDE TO CREATING A HOME YOU ADORE

BEAU CIOLINO & MATT ARMATO

Abrams, New York

DEDICATION

To Meme, Renée, and both our moms,
whose love, support, and expertise
made this book possible.

Contents

Introduction

Welcome to an all-encompassing guide to casual domesticity, by the lovable gay couple who has built a career out of making homemaking approachable. That's us! On our blog, *Probably This*, and now in this here book, we give you all the tools you need to make your home feel full of life (no matter how vacant you may be on the inside!). If you'd told us when we first started our adventure together nine years ago that people would be reading a book about innovative homemaking that *we* wrote, we'd have stared blankly at you from our messy, leaky attic apartment and rolled our eyes. But a lot has changed since then, and we want to share all of that growth with you!

So, what does "all-encompassing" . . . encompass? We think of attainable homemaking as having three major tiers: putting intention into your home's aesthetic and function (Part 1: Design), using your own two hands to make your place uniquely yours (Part 2: DIY), and honing your hosting skills to make your guests say, "Wow, that's . . . that's really nice" (Part 3: Entertaining).

Interesting spaces, handmade and heartfelt touches, and a table set with good food and drinks—all of that comes together to support the memories we make with friends, family, and—hell, maybe even strangers, we're not your parents. We're here to show you how to live your best, most beautiful, and fulfilling home life while dealing with the limitations that come with renting, working long hours, and/or not having a lot of expendable income—all of which applied to us when we first started. And even if it doesn't apply to you and never has, we think we've still got some tips you could use.

Here are a few things you can expect from this book:

1 We won't be giving long dissertations on color theory, impractical DIY projects that no normal human wants to do, or lengthy cocktail recipes where you have to, like, flambé something. We're cutting the fat and getting straight to the basic needs of a home—that it's comfortable for you and suited to welcome the people you love, with, okay, some wow factors here and there.

2 The projects within this book are curated for renters and homeowners alike. Some of our projects may not be realistic for everybody or every home, but where possible we've offered alternatives for people who are limited by either budget or lease restrictions.

3 We're oversimplifying basically everything we tell you here because, well, we're self-taught jacks-of-all-trades, not specialists. If you're an expert in any of the fields we're covering, thank you for joining us, and we're sorry for whatever thing we bastardized, but please do not worry about sending an email.

4 To keep this journey into the world of homemaking as approachable as possible, we're introducing you to some key terms that will be useful in further exploring the projects and concepts this book touches on. Whenever you see something **STYLED LIKE THIS**, that's lingo you can easily research online or use in conversation with a professional in that field, such as wine terms like **CÔTES DU RHÔNE** and paint finishes like **SEMI-GLOSS**.

Now if you're along for the ride, it feels like a good time to tell you just a little more about us and the places we've called home, which have each shaped our approach to homemaking.

Our Story

We started dating in college (Beau saw Matt first; Matt said hello first), and we moved in together irresponsibly fast. Our first place was Beau's small apartment just off campus that had musty stained carpet and a sloped ceiling that made you feel like you were in someone's attic . . . because it was actually an attic, haphazardly renovated by a money-grubbing real estate development company. Everything between us was just dandy, but everything around us made us want to die. We made the most of what we had, reorganizing our Target throw pillows, carefully building cheese boards from the "under $4" bucket at Whole Foods, and tinkering with cocktail recipes.

As much as we tried, that first home together was pretty unremarkable. We had a lot of growing to do if we were going to blossom into the domestic angels we'd always dreamed of being. Beau, growing up, would waltz down the aisles of Michaels crafts store to attend baking and cake decorating classes. When he was a preteen and his parents remarried, he put his skills on display by making his mom's wedding cake and his dad's groom cake. Each was a hit. Matt always had an interest in decor and design, solidified by a childhood trip to Graceland and an argument with his grandmother (a lifelong antiques collector and interior designer) about the merits of the green shag carpet in Elvis's Jungle Room. She expressed physical discomfort at the gaudy design choices there; Matt had a minor epiphany that decor boundaries existed to be broken.

We took on extra shifts at our jobs (late nights in swanky restaurants) and ditched the dingy apartment. Our next home was a modern apartment that felt fresh and new with an industrial edge to it, with a small loft bedroom and a large, high-ceilinged entertaining

space. It became the perfect place for us to really dive into our interests in decorating and hosting. We curated our first home bar and then drank through it way too fast. We planned small, cozy gatherings and threw the occasional party—experimenting with tablescapes and mood lighting to set the tone for a relaxing evening of gossiping about all the people we didn't invite.

That's the apartment where, late one night, the idea for a blog came around. Neither of us was sure what our post-college lives would look like, but the future didn't look very promising, and neither of us had the talent

or drive to pursue any traditional career paths. We took stock of our mutual love for home decor, kitchen things, and entertaining, combined with Beau's burgeoning interest in photography and Matt's experience as a writing tutor—and it felt like we had everything we needed to start a blog. At first it was just a side project to share recipes and decorating ideas with our friends and family, but it quickly became an all-consuming documentation of our lives and our journey in homemaking. And, for reasons we're still unsure of, a bunch of people besides just our moms started paying attention, which felt kind of nice!

We named the blog *Probably This*, because it captured our flippant "We're figuring it out!" approach to homemaking. What do you need for a better home? *shrug* Probably this? It also finally helped us answer the most anxiety-producing question in the world: What are you doing after college? "Probably this" became our response. We spent our days redecorating rooms, practicing photography, testing recipes, and writing for our newfound online community. In the evening we'd go into our restaurant jobs, learning everything we could about creating moods, crafting cocktails, and pairing wine—often getting off at 2:00 A.M. and doing it over again the next day.

After a couple of years experimenting and blogging in our little loft apartment, we decided to expand our surroundings by looking for a bigger home with a little more room to breathe. A quick scan on Craigslist produced a bright pink shotgun home that made us both drool—we toured and started our lease that same week. When you live in a house that is painted bubblegum pink, it feels less unhinged, maybe even appropriate, to decorate the interior with the same level of intensity. So we did, and we've brought a similar level of flair to all our subsequent homes, not thinking twice about splattering walls with colors like ochre and turquoise and peach. Around this time, we realized that if we really pinched our pennies we could blog, like, as a career. It wasn't the most responsible decision, but back then our dynamic tended to look like unconditional reinforcement of each other's risky long-shot ideas. So, we quit our jobs and started focusing all our professional energy into making home lifestyle content for the internet.

It was still just a few years into our relationship, but here we were committing not only to one another but also to a business and a "brand." It should've been scary or overwhelming, but to be honest, it was awesome.

So, with hearts full of hope and wallets that were completely empty, we turned to secondhand, vintage, and DIY elements to make our deranged, grandiose visions

come to life—notably learning that sometimes, if you ask nicely, many landlords are cool with you changing things like paint colors and light fixtures (see page 52).

We loved the pink house, but all good things come to an end, and our time there was up as soon as we laid eyes on a 1969 Globestar camper trailer named Rosie and decided a totally irresponsible adventure was in order. Sensing a theme?

Rosie was in rough shape, so we spent a hot summer DIYing our way through a camper renovation, teaching ourselves how to lay tile and build countertops and refurbish cabinetry—and also how *not* to do all of those things. Once she was all dolled up, we sold everything we owned and packed up our lives for three months of travel out West. We found inspiration in the adobe-style homes of Santa Fe, toured wineries up and down California, and learned all the ways to make living in a small box of a home not horrible. We got by on the slow trickle of spon-con jobs for our blog and stretched our money by only eating at restaurants with questionable health ratings. After three months of travel, we checked our bank account, let out a blood-curdling scream, and decided the sun had set on this adventure.

We hightailed it back to Louisiana and, with no lease or plan, ended up staying a few weeks at Beau's mom's house in the small town of Covington—home to swamps, cargo pants, and maybe three gay people, if you count our dog, Fox. And we kind of fell in love with it. It was quiet, and simple, and a nice break from months of being on the road. Also, it had cheap rentals (which was great because we had no money left). We wound up leasing a small open-concept unit in a sterile new-build apartment complex, and it became our blank slate.

We worked through tough questions like "How many vintage pieces are too many?" (N/A) and "Can you just make your own paint color by mixing together two paints?" (yes, if they're the same base and finish). We made our cookie-cutter apartment feel unique and homey, even though it was off the highway, behind a few car dealerships. We experimented with designating spaces in an open-concept floor plan (see page 61), and how to make a room feel inspired even when its surroundings were very much uninspired. A small, generic apartment in the middle of nowhere became our cozy cocoon of a home and the birthplace of some of our most favorite projects, like our online shop—filled with items like scented candles, and totes with our "Better Homo & Garden" tagline— and it was even where we first imagined writing this book.

We think of each home as an essential part of our life story, and we've made it a priority to make them all as pleasant and perfect-for-us as possible. After spending those two years laying low in that small apartment, we saved enough money for a down payment on our first home purchase and have been tirelessly renovating it while writing this book. But we're saving major renovation material for the next volume!

This book is here to help you refine, explore, and expand your homemaking skills, whether you own or rent, and whether you have a big budget or none at all. We hope that with every new place you call home, you'll turn to it to help guide and inspire you, because if we can go from clueless college garbage to gunning for Martha Stewart's crown and scepter, dear god you can too.

PART 1

Design

Vintage finds highlighted against modern backdrops, androgynous blends of movement and color, and enough plants to make you forget you were having a rough day—that's probably the shortest way we could possibly describe our design aesthetic. But whether or not our style appeals to you, the real heart of our design philosophy is approachability, individuality, and comfort. Neither of us has formal interior design training, but we've got lots of experience in bringing blah spaces to life through thoughtful and individualized design, without a massive budget. Here's where that starts.

CHAPTER 1

Our Design Philosophy: Make It Look Like People Live Here

We're not huge fans of pigeonholing our aesthetic with typical industry descriptors. We try to pull inspiration from many different sources, and they often don't fall within just one certain category or aesthetic. We think that's the most tried-and-true approach to designing a home that feels timeless and unique—combining elements of several different styles into a singular cohesive space that makes you feel right at home.

The most important thing to us when designing a space is to make it look well-loved and lived-in—basically, make it look like a thoughtfully curated home, not a museum—and to match the aesthetic choices to the personality of whoever lives there: Make it look like *your* home.

So, can we tell you a secret? Whenever we start designing a space, we usually have no clue what it's going to actually look like. Sure, we may have some kind of obscure idea in mind, like, "backstage dressing room in *The Birdcage*" or "Solange's 'Cranes in the Sky' music video, a minute and twenty-eight seconds in," but the priority consideration is figuring out what we want a space to *feel* like for daily use. Once you have that, then you can start working from the back end, designing for utility and comfort while incorporating pieces, patterns, colors, and textures that will bring you that feeling.

Picking a Vibe:
Your Starting Point

So, how do you want the room to feel? Don't limit yourself—there's no budget for this step, and it doesn't require some kind of innate designer know-how or advanced skill set. This is technically the easiest part, but it's also the most important because it's going to be your GPS throughout the entire design process. Take some time, think of some of your favorite spaces, places where you've felt whatever vibe you want to achieve—whether it's been in your current home, previous homes, friends' homes, or even hotels you've stayed in—and narrow down your adjectives.

An office we designed recently started with us wanting a room that felt "stately" and "contemplative." So, we went with a bold navy color, high arched bookshelves, and decorative molding that screamed Victorian study melodrama, because, well, those design decisions fit the designated vibe (see pages 34–35).

The living room pictured here started as a small, cold corner of an apartment, but we wanted it to feel youthful, organic, and inviting. By combining bold colors, natural fibers, and pieces both new and old, we created a comfortable space that hits all those marks.

Designing for Your Life: Considering Utility

Home design is not the time to lie to yourself! A beautifully designed room doesn't mean anything if you're never going to use it or won't fully enjoy your time there. This isn't a "beauty is pain" moment. Your home is the place for you to feel most comfortable! So, let's not fit our way of life into the designs we love, and instead fit the designs we love into our way of life.

In every place we've lived together, we had what we like to call an Entryway Crap Drawer. When we walk into the house with things we don't want or need but shouldn't get rid of (like a letter from the IRS asking for that forty-seven dollars we still owe from 2017, *again*), it all just goes right in the crap drawer until one of us gets the guts to go through and deal with the backlog. Had we tried to design our homes based on who we wanted to be (people who opened and then paid their bills upon receiving them and then immediately recycled the paper) instead of who we are (people who put that shit off until we start getting threatening phone calls), we'd have bills all over the place.

Taking the time to consider how you use any given space—whether it's just your bedroom in a shared apartment or each of the rooms in your home—is key to figuring out your plan for making it oh so adorable.

Simple questions can help guide your own understanding of how you use a space, like:

1 What piece of living room furniture has the biggest Netflix dent? (Yes, this is from your butt.)

2 What surface in your home has the most clutter?

3 Which part of your home do you most enjoy being in? And which part of your home do you avoid the most?

4 Where do you naturally gather with two or three friends? Five or more friends?

5 Will this book be displayed proudly on your coffee table? Please?

Here, look, we'll help by showing how answers to these questions can spark design solutions:

1. What piece of living room furniture has the biggest Netflix dent?

Fill this space with assorted pillows and a blanket that you love, a small shrine of sorts to your favorite part of the living room that you'll curl up in every evening (yes, this will also help cover the crater you've created). Place a side table within reach to hold your favorite scented candle and a glass of wine.

2. What surface in your home has the most clutter?

Consider making your clutter a part of your design. In one of our past apartments, the living area had ample surface space—a coffee table, a small bookshelf, and an end table. Do you know where any books we were flipping through always ended up? On the floor by the sofa. So rather than fight against our slob nature, we put a small jute sitting mat on the floor by the couch, arranged a few big and beautiful books on it, and it became our "current reading pile," which didn't look so out of place (pictured on page 109). We were already using this area that way, so why not lean into it and make the design of the room work for our messy lifestyle? Something as simple as an antique brass tray or a woven basket placed on or near your most clutter-prone surface can house your items and keep your space feeling tidy.

3. Which part of your home do you most enjoy being in? And which part of your home do you avoid the most?

When we hit a stopping point with work for the day and have no energy left, we have a *very* steep decline. We need a calming and neat bedroom to retreat to, and so even when the rest of the house is a wreck because of a renovation or just run-of-the-mill depression that comes about every so often, we treat our favorite room with the utmost respect; the bed is always made, and the room clear of clutter. At the end of the day, when we walk in and see a gorgeous headboard wall, plush bedding, properly placed throw pillows, and precisely dimmed mood lighting, we fall asleep real quick.

Maybe the best moment of your day is making a cup of coffee? Hello, create an adorable coffee area where you can give a demure smile to the camera after that first steamy sip like every coffee commercial ever. Whether that means arranging your coffee and mugs in an intentional pattern, or turning a bar cart into a coffee station that's decked out and highlighted by a piece of art hung on the wall behind it, prioritize the moments that are already your favorite, and work from there.

As for the part of the house you can't stand, why aren't you using it? Is it awkwardly out of the way or hard to get to? Aesthetically pleasing storage may just be your answer! Are you one of the lucky few with more space than they need? Frivolous non-functional decor can bring quirk and personality to a space! Dig into the meaningless pleasures you find in life. Maybe that's where you need a vintage arcade game machine, peacock statue, or a bust atop a column.

4. Where do you naturally gather with two or three friends? Five or more friends?

Do you really have five friends??? Popular. If having friends over is as important to you as it is to us (whether it's a genuine love of being hospitable or because you just never want to leave your house), you've probably noticed where folks tend to congregate. Is that something you should lean into or push against? If the space feels cramped by the immovable parts of your home like walls and permanent fixtures, you can use design and spatial rearrangements to entice folks to an alternate area. The coziest, most comfortable spots to post up are pockets where you're not interrupting the flow of other people moving around you— make sure those pockets are dressed up and ready to welcome your guests.

5. Will this book be displayed proudly on your coffee table? Please?

It's totally fine if not; just wanted to float the idea! That being said, we love artfully displaying the things we use the most (whether it be this book, other books, liquor collections, or even fashion accessories like hats and bags) and weaving them into our design aesthetic for a room.

These are just a handful of the many things to consider about how you live. Whether you're putting together a design plan for a single room or your entire house, think through your daily routines and habits, consider how you use your home, and make sure these things are considered and even prioritized when planning your design.

Now that you know what you want a space to *feel* like, and you've had a long and honest conversation with yourself about *how* you live in a space, it's time to take those considerations, coupled with the knowledge of what strengths and limitations your space has, and turn them into choosing the actual component pieces. And to be honest with you, it's not always so easy. This is why interior designers and decorators have jobs. But hiring those people costs money, which . . . who has that? With a little bit of planning and effort, this is something you're 100 percent capable of doing yourself. We believe in you!

MOOD BOARD TO MOCK-UP TO MAKING IT HAPPEN

The next three chapters dive into the steps we use to design everything from small spaces like a dining nook to large-scale projects like a bedroom suite remodel. We hope you take these steps, adapt them to your own needs, and use them to make your place real cute.

CHAPTER 2

Creating a Mood Board: Honing Your Design Direction, the Lazy Way

When planning your space, it may feel good to declare a specific design direction, such as **MID-CENTURY MODERN** or **FARMHOUSE** or **GLAM**. If that's served you in the past feel free to stick to that approach. But you don't need to pigeonhole yourself into one design style or trend. In the following section we dive further into how to establish the design direction for a particular room, and over time, your general aesthetic preferences will naturally reveal themselves. Well, that's the goal, at least!

We're not going to give you some "ten steps to success" mandate. What we'll give you is the simple, accessible, and, yes, kind of lazy method of creating a space that has helped us plan dozens of designs spanning a multitude of budgets.

Your starting point is, well, Pinterest. Sure, if you're like an old-school neurotic type, you could print out individual images of rooms you like and pin them all onto a wall while pounding cold brew and frantically making notes on each image. But we really just recommend Pinterest, the tool that democratized home design for so many and allowed us to explore and expand our very own taste. You'll see us reference the app a few times in this book, as it's how we often start planning a space. Filling a "board" with designs or design elements you love is a great way to pinpoint, well, what you love.

There's a misconception that Pinterest is just loaded with clickbait design porn, and sure, there's a lot of that. But with a discerning eye, critical thinking, and proper searches, you can root out all of the "made-for-Pinterest" spaces and find design ideas that are both exciting and realistic. You can find historic designs, tried-and-true traditional designs, and, yes, more cutting-edge and popular-now stuff all on Pinterest.

We can already see the negative Amazon reviews: "These guys just told me to use Pinterest to design my home, what a waste of money, gay people *are* bad!" Well, sometimes the most useful tools are the most obvious, *if*

you know how to use them. Years ago, we'd take on occasional photography and staging jobs to afford food and health care and other sweet, sweet American privileges. On one job, there was a very well-respected and, uhhh, rich New Orleans–area interior designer working on set, and guess what was pulled up on her laptop? Pinterest. Loads of Pinterest boards, each labeled with different client homes she was working on. Point being, you have access to some of the same tools as the pros, so let's use them, okay?

Create a Pinterest board for the space you're planning, and add things to it by searching for the vibe descriptors you've

LOCAL VIBES

Taking cues from your surroundings is key to creating a space that feels intuitive and "right." The bright pink home we lived in a few years ago inspired our love of color. What parts of your surroundings do you love? Is your neighborhood filled with jewel-colored and ornate Victorian homes? Large oak trees that cast shadows and calm? Cherry blossoms that bring joy with every blooming season? How can you bring that into your home decor?

selected on page 20, plus the type of space you're creating—"stately office" or "tidy bathroom," or, if you already have a color direction or other aspect in mind, add that to the mix: "calming sage bedroom" or "elegant tropical dining room."

You can pin full rooms as inspo, or individual items you're drawn to. Furniture pieces, textures, fabrics, materials, cabinet pulls, wallpapers, colors, light fixtures, art, and other decorative pieces can all be added to your board. Go as concrete or abstract as you want here. Maybe you pin a product photo of an exact chair from Pottery Barn, or maybe you pin a surreal fashion photo because you like the colors, patterns, or even the attitude of the model.

Pin to your heart's desire on that board—Pinterest's algorithm is incredible, and once you start selecting things you like it's going to do most of the work for you by finding similar spaces to force-feed you. Gobble it up. If there's something you want to have in the design, but you don't come across it on Pinterest, do a quick Google image search and add it to your board manually. Then, when you're kinda over it, go ahead and edit. Remove all the things that make you say, "Why did I pin this?" and take a good hard look at your board. Note the patterns that emerge, or if a certain color is prevalent, or a fabric or texture. Is this board giving you what you were originally aiming for? If so, awesome. If not, it's time to

WORK WITH WHAT YOU'VE GOT

When crafting your aesthetic, make sure you include the pieces you already own that you'd like to use! Take a photo of your coffee table, for example, and upload it to your Pinterest board just to visualize it with everything you'll be adding. Make sure you're shooting in bright but indirect natural light for the best representation of the piece.

adjust your search terms to get closer to what you originally wanted. Alternatively, if you find yourself gravitating toward the unexpected, follow that instinct. Part of creating a space you love is herding it as it wanders and roams.

When you feel like you've reached a stopping point, take some time away from your board so you can revisit it with fresh eyes. You may notice themes you hadn't previously ("Who knew I loved black velvet!"), or a pattern might emerge that you want to steer clear of ("Why is everything black velvet?").

Now that you've started to hone your design direction, our next chapter will take you from your conceptual Pinterest vision board to a more literal representation of the space you're creating. Seatbelts, everyone!

CHAPTER 3

Making a Mock-Up: Finessing the Vision

Now that we have our Pinterest mood board under way, it's time to use elements from that mood board to create a basic digital rendering of your space. And look, we know that sounds like a lot of effort, but it really doesn't have to be— this can be as rudimentary or fleshed out as you have the time and energy for. You don't need to be proficient in any fancy design software to mock up what your dream space will look like. In fact, while we sometimes utilize design apps to flesh out a mock-up, most of the time we stick to good old-fashioned sketching by hand plus some simple digitizations to compile images, fabrics, colors, and patterns to see if the jumble of ideas in our mood board translates well when laid out in a literal expression of the space.

With a pretty limited Photoshop skill level, you can arrange photos of all your objects and edit them using Photoshop's "Transform" tools to resize, rotate, and stretch the objects. If you want to go the extra mile and add depth and perspective to your mock-up, you can even play with the "Skew" and "Distort" tools to change the shape of, say, a rug to give it some dimension and feel like you're actually looking into the room. If Photoshop isn't an option for you, there are some free or cheap programs that can be helpful—affordable options like Procreate for iPad allow you to freely sketch and easily make adjustments to different elements of your mock-up. Morpholio Board has an easy-to-use background-eraser feature to help you place, say, a coffee table seamlessly on top of a rug without displaying the white background of an online product photo. There are also free options like web-based Photopea, a nearly perfect replacement for Photoshop. SketchUp is a higher-end software that's still user-friendly and ideal for more detailed 3-D mock-ups—making renderings that are to scale is a more time-consuming step but can be really helpful in visualizing how objects' sizes and proportions work together. And, hey, if you do happen to be artistically inclined or just work most comfortably on paper, sketching your ideas out by hand is totally an option here.

APP/PROGRAM	COST	PLATFORM	NOTES
Photoshop	$$	Desktop, free mobile version	Our preferred software for creating mock-ups
Morpholio Board	$	Mobile	User-friendly design app great for anyone new to creating mock-ups and sketches
Color 911	$	Mobile	Interior decorating app that allows you to create and organize color palettes
Procreate	$	iPad only	Illustration app great for sketching design plans
Photopea	Free	Web	Web-based photo editor with many of the same tools as Photoshop
SketchUp	$$$	Web, desktop	Advanced software for anyone wanting to create detailed and proportional 3-D mock-ups

Once you've narrowed down your desires for a space by editing down your mood board, you can begin ordering product samples for things like window treatments, paints, wallpapers, stains, tiles, fabric, etc. to see how different colors, textures, and materials work together IRL. For a specific piece that you can't get a sample of, use what you can find without ordering the full piece itself, like a 4-inch (10 cm) piece of aged brass to stand in for a light fixture you're considering, or a marble tile that represents the marble coffee table you're eyeing. You'll at least get an idea of how the color and texture of the object will work with the other elements.

Programs like SketchUp can be used to create incredibly detailed renderings of a space, allowing you to account for how natural light will illuminate certain colors and textures, or how shadows will fall. More advanced programs like this obvi aren't necessary but can be a useful tool for all you perfectionists out there.

As you see physical samples of your different elements, you can go back to your digital mock-up to alter or adjust as needed. Like, if you get your paint sample on the wall and realize you absolutely hate everything about it, it's simple to change the colors in your digital mock-up to a second choice and see how you feel about all the other pieces' ability to work. As you develop the design, you can start to get more detailed with your mock-up, adding vases, candles, plants, and other small finishing touches.

Once you've finalized everything you want to use in your design, the next step is the big one—making it happen!!

EDIT EARLY AND OFTEN

Our initial design for our home office included a terrazzo desk, peacock wallpaper, and tufted velvet ceiling, which felt fun and bold, but as we sat with the mock-up it began to feel too chaotic to be the "stately" and "contemplative" workspace we set out to create. While we kept most of the elements in place, like the shape, size, and color of the bookshelves, a digital mock-up helped us edit the plan early on to define a clearer direction. A more traditional desk, a solid fabric background for the shelves, and a mature plaid ceiling treatment fit the vibe much better.

CHAPTER 4

Making It Happen: A Beginner's Guide to Furnishing Your Place

Congrats on making it past the planning stages! Now it's time to make it all happen by shopping, moving your pieces into place, and crossing your fingers that it all looks just as good IRL. If you've planned thoroughly, maybe you'll be completely satisfied—but more than likely, even with the most meticulous design outline, you may find yourself making edits up to the last minute. That's okay! Embrace this natural evolution, and let the space wander as it wants to.

Once you've gone through creating a mood board and a mock-up, the final step is gathering together pieces you already own, shopping for any new pieces you may need, and implementing your vision! Shopping for your new empty apartment, or even for just a sofa, can be overwhelming, but we're here to hopefully make it much less awful. Taking notes to help you remember ideas you love, organize projects you want to do, and keep track of shopping lists isn't a terrible idea!

The more thought you've put into your mood board and mock-up, the easier this process will be. You can take a step back at any point in this journey, returning to the mood board stage or the mock-up stage if anything feels wrong once you dive in.

Step 1: Ever-Growing Project

Accept the fact that your space and home will constantly be changing, and you may never feel "done." If you've put pressure on yourself to find everything all at once, remove that pressure: The best furniture collections are built over time, and the best home designs are able to adapt and change as your tastes and needs shift over the course of your life. Also, you put too much pressure on yourself as it is, so don't add to it, sweetie. Your home should be a place of relaxation, and that includes the experience of designing it as well as living in it.

Step 2: Taking Inventory

Make a list of everything you currently own, including the items you don't love. Consider whether any of it can be refreshed or repurposed (page 103 can help with this!), or if it needs to be replaced. Can you actually paint that old nightstand and turn it into a side table for your living room? Does that IKEA cabinet just need new knobs to feel less, well, IKEA? What do you need to actually purchase new, and what holes need to be filled with styling and other decor? Being careful to consider every single thing you may need, build a list of new (or, new to you) items to shop for.

Look at the sofa in the first picture. It's a pretty unremarkable beige sofa. That's okay, though—just because the sofa is the biggest piece of furniture in the room, that doesn't mean it has to be the star. Check out how the room in the next photo utilizes that same sofa but adds texture and color variation to give the space character in a way a beige sofa can't do on its own. If you've got a basic piece of furniture that may no longer suit your style, don't rush to get rid of it without first dressing it up with items that fit your current taste. It just might surprise you!

Step 3: Budget (Ugh, Sorry!)

Assess your money situation and decide how much you can reasonably spend on each item. Allow yourself a small contingency—10 to 20 percent of your budget—to tap into if you find the *perfect piece*, but otherwise *stick to that budget*, 'cause we're going out for tacos and margaritas after.

Step 4: Shop Until You've Filled the Void

Not an emotional void, hon! We can't help you with that, and neither will furniture. Armed with your items list, budget, and design plan, it's time to shop! If you haven't yet, use a tape measure to get an accurate measurement of your space. If you're working with a tight budget and/or want to add charm, all while being environmentally friendly, your starting point is vintage and consignment shops (the chapter titled "Repairing and Refurbishing Vintage Furniture Pieces," on page 99, has a good briefer on shopping secondhand!).

Want to freshen up a space with brand-new pieces? Consider design-forward brands that offer items at mid-range prices, like **ARHAUS, ROVE CONCEPTS, LULU & GEORGIA, ANTHROPOLOGIE HOME, INTERIOR DEFINE, JOYBIRD, CB2, BALLARD DESIGNS, APT 2B, PERIGOLD, WEST ELM, ARTICLE, NOVOGRATZ**, and **LIVING SPACES**. If you're shopping for pieces online, particularly large furniture, check the dimensions and use these measurements to tape out each piece, ensuring it's a good fit. This is a super-simple process that just involves using painter's tape to mark a piece's dimensions on the floor, giving you an idea of how it'll fit in a room in proximity to other pieces you own or plan to buy. Want a budget tip? Find a piece you love and do a web search for when that brand or store typically has its big yearly or quarterly sale, and wait to make your purchase then—many big stores put the same or similar categories on sale at the same time from year to year, so it's easy to look ahead with a little internet detective work.

We love combining old and new pieces to bring together charm and modern comfort to a room, but the more you browse for pieces, the better idea you'll get of what you like.

VINTAGE VULTURES

One of our absolute favorite ways to shop is vintage and consignment, and you're going to see us bring it up *a lot*. We love the hunt for vintage pieces and the character they can bring into a room—not to mention that buying used pieces is environmentally friendly and usually more affordable than buying new pieces, and they're often made with higher-quality materials meant to last (like real wood versus the engineered wood and particleboard so often used today!). If we find a secondhand piece we absolutely adore, it can help inform the rest of the design direction for a space.

Consignment shopping at Consign Consign in New Orleans

Furniture That Fits

What was that? You've got no clue what size your furniture should be? Aw, crap . . . Okay, let's get into it.

Sofa

What sofa length is best for your space? To sectional or not to sectional? Standard sofa lengths vary from about 70 to more than 100 inches (1.8 to 2.5 m) and choosing the right one is dependent on the size and flow of your room. An undersized sofa can make a room feel smaller or uninviting, while something too large will look clunky, so, let's just aim for that sweet spot. Shop around and tape out different lengths (or shapes) of sofas that call out to you and see which best fits the space and flow, making sure you're also accounting for any side tables you might be placing on either end. Don't forget to consider the depth! A seat depth of 20 to 23 inches (50 to 57.5 cm) is ideal to sit in for a standard sofa, especially if your space is super tight, but if you want to lounge? Let's kick that up to 26 inches (66 cm) for a proper space to curl up in. As for whether or not to sectional, that's a personal lifestyle choice that we're fine with as long as you keep it behind closed doors and don't shove it in our faces! We think sectionals can be great when they fit the size and mood of a room.

Accent Chairs

Accent chairs do so much more than just add space for butts! They can be used to amp up a room's style, fill out blank space, and maybe most importantly, designate a living space as a spot for entertaining, not just a spot to watch TV. When you style a living room with just a sofa facing a TV, you pretty much assign that room to TV duty—and when you try and sit in said room with friends for cocktails and a goss-goss session you'll notice that big empty black box still sucks in all the attention, because you've designed it that way. *No bueno.* Accent chairs placed opposite a sofa or facing each other on opposite sides of a coffee table can help keep the room's focus away from the TV wall and more toward the center of the room, creating a space for conversation.

If you're stuck with a sofa you don't love or a room that feels unremarkable, accent chairs can add that extra spark with something a little bolder. Whether or not they have arms is up to you; just keep in mind that armchairs are more comfortable for lounging around but will also require more space. If you're working with really limited space or a super-tight budget, dining chairs are typically less expensive and have a smaller frame—just dress them up with throws or pillows to feel comfier. As with all furniture, taping out the dimensions of the accent chairs you're eyeing is your best bet for getting a preview of how they will fit in your room. Oh! A word of caution! Living room sets—you know, the ones with a matching sofa and chairs—can sometimes be done well, but can just as easily look generic and thought-less. So, ironically enough, we often find that mismatched furniture is the easier route to a cohesive space.

Dining Table

The perfectly sized dining table is one that leaves at least 36 inches (90 cm) of space between the table and the walls, which is typically just enough room for folks to get past when the seat is occupied. Ideally you'd be able to fit at least four people at any given dining table, and we personally love a dining table with a leaf. Most of our homes have been smaller apartments with limited space for a table, so having one that could stay small when it was just us but expand for having friends over came in handy. Even if it's a bit of a tight fit with the leaf in place, it's best to have enough table surface area to share a meal. If your home has more of an open-concept floor plan with a "dining area" instead of a full dining room, check out page 61 for tips on designating space so your dining table doesn't look like it's randomly placed.

Coffee Table

Your coffee table should be no higher than the height of your sofa's seat. That's generally around 18 inches (45 cm). When picking out a size, keep in mind it should be large enough that, ideally, every seat surrounding it could reach it without much effort, but you also want it small enough so it's not blocking a path. Giving your coffee table 18 to 24 inches (46 to 60 cm) of clearance from each piece of furniture should meet these needs! As with accent chairs, coffee tables can be a smart place to add contrast to a room, either through color or material, so don't let your choice be an afterthought. See also our tips for styling a coffee table on page 74!

Beds

You're going to be most comfortable in at least a queen bed, but dang, if you have the space for a king . . . do it! Ideally any bed you choose for your room will be centered along a wall in an area where no doors or windows will fall behind the headboard with enough space for the bed to be flanked by two bedside tables. And you're going to be putting your mattress in a bed frame, not just using a mattress on the floor, okay? That only looks cute in Urban Outfitters Instagram posts, not real life. A 10 by 10-foot (3 by 3 m) room is right about the minimum you need for a queen-sized bed, and you'll want at least a 10 by 12-foot (3 by 3.6 m) room for a king bed. Queen bed frames typically run from 62 to 65 inches (1.57 to 1.65 m) wide, while king bed frames will be right around 80 inches (2 m) wide. Use these measurements plus the width of your night-stands to find the right bed for your space.

Rugs

And all of that stuff needs to go on top of something . . . enter: rugs! See the diagrams on this page and the next for general guidelines on rug and furniture placement. As for rug shopping—that's a whole art form of its own and can be particularly difficult. Here are some of our rug-shopping pointers.

If you gather nothing else from this section, we really need you to understand that an undersized rug can truly be worse than no rug at all. A rug that is too small can shrink a room, make furniture look clunky, and cause you to pace the room in a circular holding pattern muttering, "No no no this is all wrong . . . what have I done?" Let's just avoid all of those things by choosing a properly sized rug.

Your general guiding principle for selecting the right size area rug is this: It should be large enough so that it *could* contain all of the furniture you put on it, but not so big that you aren't able to leave at least 18 to 24 inches (46 to 60 cm) of space between the edge of the rug and the wall.

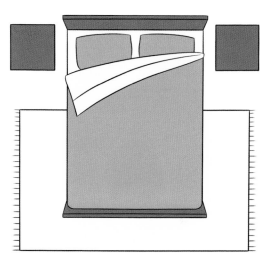

In a bedroom, an area rug should sit perpendicular to and under the foot of the bed, coming out about 24 inches (60 cm) from each side and the foot of the bed—in this orientation it will not extend to the headboard legs at all, and that's okay. (We almost always use an 8 by 10-foot [2.4 by 3 m] area rug in our bedrooms, but a larger room with a king bed can also be styled with a 9 by 12-foot [2.7 by 3.6 m] rug as long as there is adequate space between the rug and the walls). For a cute and cost-effective alternative, skip a

bedroom area rug in favor of a small rug or runner on either side of the bed. A 3 by 5-foot (1 by 1.5 m) rug works well for this, adding warmth visually and physically for your cold little toes in the morning. If you've got a unique setup or just want to be extra sure, use painter's tape to map out the outline of the rug size you're planning to purchase, and see that it fits all of the above size requirements and feels right to you before you buy.

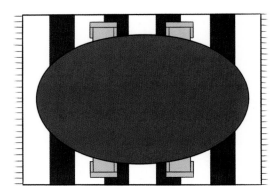

Your dining table should sit in the dead center of the rug, so that all four legs of each dining chair rest on the rug when tucked into the table (we've always had a 60-inch [152 cm] dining table and almost always use a 5 by 8-foot [1.5 by 2.4 m] rug in our dining spaces).

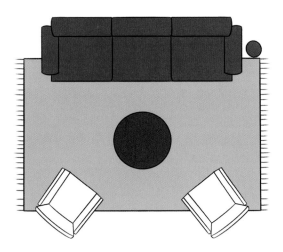

In a living room, you'll want to ground your furniture by placing at least the front two legs of any seating on an area rug (we almost always use an 8 by 10-foot [2.4 by 3 m] rug in our living spaces).

When shopping for vintage rugs, which we do a whole lot, you'll notice that many older handmade woven rugs don't follow today's typical area rug sizes (5 by 8, 8 by 10, 9 by 12 feet) and sometimes may seem totally random. In this case, careful measuring and following our guidelines above for furniture placement and distance from walls can help you make the best possible decision.

MORE ON RUGS: SHAPE, MATERIAL, STYLE, COLOR, AND PATTERN

We could write an entire book on rugs, and people have, but the music is starting to play and our time on this topic is coming to an end, so we'll leave you with our best, most succinct advice. Rectangular rugs are your best bet. Other than animal hide rugs, we typically recommend staying away from funky or irregular shapes as they tend to be trendy and less versatile (we're all about reducing waste and having to buy new pieces every time you move isn't really ideal). The exception to this is if you're using a rug for a bold accent, or if your room or furniture is round—like a circular dining table or turret-style nook—in which case a circular, oval, or asymmetrical rug may make sense.

RAPID-FIRE TIPS:

Handmade and vintage rugs tend to look timeless and can be used in a wide variety of spaces, so as with furniture, our first stop when shopping for rugs is second-hand sellers.

As for buying new pieces, there are plenty of online stores with affordable rugs that look lovely in the product shot but may look (and be) very cheap when they arrive at your doorstep. Your best bet to see how a rug actually looks in a real non-staged space is by looking at a brand's tagged photos on social media. As with everything in life, a little sleuthing goes a long way!

Consider the utility of the rug when thinking about color and material. For example, entryways do best with rugs made of dark, synthetic materials that are easily cleaned, or something hardy like jute that can handle a little wear and tear. Bedrooms are an ideal place to go with something nice and plush and to avoid any coarse fibers that aren't pleasant to step on barefoot.

CHAPTER 5

Colors That Feel Like Home: The Right Shades for Your Place

Here are just some of the lies you've been told: Yellow causes anxiety, dark colors make rooms feel smaller, and a college degree will help you succeed in life. While those ideas can *sometimes* be true, they are not hard-and-fast rules, and they've been keeping you from happiness. We promise. In this chapter we're here to guide you on choosing colors around your home, from paint, to decor, to the color of furniture and your finishing touches.

We're exploring everything from wall color, to the color of the fabric on your furniture, to the colors of the small decorative pieces you choose to style with. When working through this chapter, and making decisions on color in your home, we encourage you to keep in mind how all those elements will work together before making final judgment calls on any one color. Maybe you don't typically gravitate toward a turquoise wall color, but in the context of the furniture you're planning to use and the decor you've got on hand, it's the perfect fit for the vibe you're creating. Treat a room's color story like a puzzle, with each item relying on the next to make it all work together.

The Right Shade: Paint

Everybody knows that paint is the quickest (and often cheapest) way to completely transform a room, but if you pick the wrong color, that transformation could end up being for the worse. The gray-pocalypse of the late 2010s demonstrated how even safe colors can be used in a way that makes you feel very . . . unsafe. Like an entire home painted gray. It's chilling.

In fact, for quick reference, please refer to our incredibly scientific "Color Alignment Chart" for some insight.

CAN I PAINT AS A RENTER? SHOULD I?

For legal reasons we're just gonna say that you're obliged to do whatever is in your lease and your landlord can 100 percent hold you responsible for breaking any of the terms, including the one that says, "Hey, don't paint this place, boo-boo." However, calling on our own personal experience, we've successfully asked several landlords to alter the language in a rental agreement to let us paint as long as the color is returned back to its previous shade prior to moving out, and we always get that exchange in writing. This includes getting the name of the existing paint color and finish to make sure you can match it.

Is your landlord horrible to speak to and you'd rather ask for forgiveness than permission? We've been there, and done that, too. Not saying you should. Just that we have. So that's that on *can* you paint as a renter.

But *should* you? Is it worth the time and money? Let's, like, crunch some numbers. Painting a room yourself costs anywhere from seventy-five to two hundred dollars, depending on the kind of tools and paint you buy. From shopping to painting to cleaning, you'll spend about eight hours total painting a room. Say you live somewhere for two years; that's 17,520 hours of living there. Just eight hours and roughly one hundred dollars, one time, maybe twice if you have to paint it back—in our opinion, that's so worth it for a room that'll feel much more like *your own*. If that's not worth it to you, there are still plenty of other ways to customize your space, and in this chapter we dive into other places where color shows up.

If you'd like to jump to our chapter all about the technical aspects of painting, including how to do it, selecting finishes, and what and where to buy, head to page 87.

The Official *Probably This* Color Alignment Chart

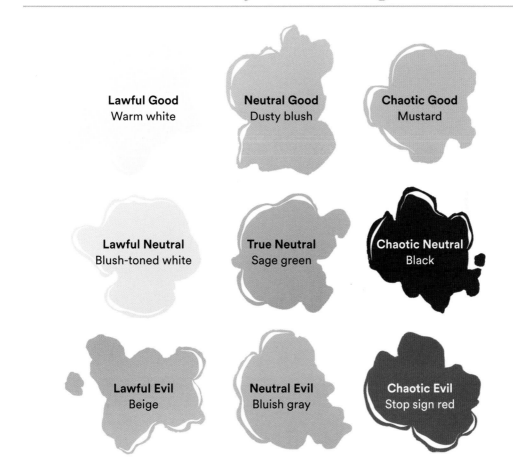

Lawful Good
Warm white

Neutral Good
Dusty blush

Chaotic Good
Mustard

Lawful Neutral
Blush-toned white

True Neutral
Sage green

Chaotic Neutral
Black

Lawful Evil
Beige

Neutral Evil
Bluish gray

Chaotic Evil
Stop sign red

As you can clearly see above, the lawful-to-chaotic axis is mostly about how saturated the color is, and the good-to-evil axis is more about how much it does or doesn't remind us of hospitals. And this, to be clear, is just according to *our* preferences and aesthetic. Feel free to develop your own chart if it would help you better grasp what colors you can always lean on, and which ones you'll thank yourself for avoiding.

Over time, the more rooms you paint and the more spaces you transform, the more comfortable you'll be with this process, but we're going to give you some basic guidelines.

As with our tips on narrowing down a room's full aesthetic, one of the most helpful tools in picking a paint color is to just spend time scanning rooms on Pinterest to start narrowing down what you like. Pin everything you love and see if there's a color or group of colors that emerges. Are there a lot of bright and bold colors? Are there a lot of warm tones happening? Is everything bright and white? Is dark and moody more your style?

When picking a paint color, consider the natural light a room gets. We recommend leaning into what a room is already doing—if there's tons of natural light, we like to lean into light and bright colors that will amp that up. If there's not very much light, we lean into moodier darker hues. You may have heard that you should avoid using darker colors in rooms that get little natural light or are small in size, but we actually see this as an opportunity to make a space that feels cozy, intimate, and maybe even a little sexy, which is sometimes just how a room wants to be! But the *amount* of light is just the starting point; you also want to consider the *kind* of light you're getting: cool or warm. Assuming there's nothing

blocking the window, or some large building isn't reflecting light into your home, north-facing windows will get cooler-hued light, while south-facing windows will lean warm (opposite in the Southern Hemisphere!). As with the above, we *generally* recommend leaning into those hues by choosing cooler tones for cooler light and warmer for warmer.

In one of our favorite pink rooms—because, yes, there have been several—we went with a coral color that allowed the warm sunlight to bounce around the room and create the most beautiful glow that changed throughout the day. Given it was a room with a south-facing window, it provided the perfect opportunity to play into the warm, bright sunlight.

If you've got a historic home or live in a historic neighborhood, or if you have a historic home style (like an early-1900s **CRAFTSMAN**), you can let history do the work and find out what palettes or colors would've traditionally been used in your home. We're not saying this should limit you to those colors, but it might give you inspiration and a starting point, as well as direct you toward colors that "feel right."

We love exciting our visitors with over-the-top designs in the areas they'll be in most, so we use bolder colors in living rooms, guest bathrooms, and dining areas. For bedrooms, we often pick something more serene and earthy. Bold colors inspire a flow of energy and conversation when we have friends over, and a calming palette in a bedroom provides low stimuli for relaxation.

REASONS TO LEAVE THOSE WALLS WHITE

Maybe we haven't mentioned it yet: We love big, bold colors! But that doesn't mean a bright wall color is always the answer!

Do you find white to just be so refreshing, calming, and beautiful?

White-out to your heart's content. Some of our favorite interiors lean heavy into white and neutrals, so we fully support it, if that's what you love. If you want to take white to a dramatic "wow" level, that can still be achieved through monochromatic color schemes, or even picking out a high-gloss finish for your paint.

Is your furniture bright and multicolored? Do you own tons of pillows, throws, art, and decor in bright colors?

You might need those white walls to provide some balance. White walls are secretly a color lover's best weapon—the stark contrast can help your colorful pieces pop.

Does the idea of painting a room a color anything other than white make you incredibly nervous?

Too bad, fear is dumb, and that's not a good enough excuse.

Sample Test Like a Designer, Darling

Once you've narrowed it down to a handful of specific colors—whether it's several shades of a similar color or a few completely different colors—it's time to get to testing. You can buy 4-ounce (120 ml) paint samples at a home improvement store for, like, five bucks, which is a worthwhile investment in making sure you end up with a color you love. Test all the samples, and then literally just stare at the wall. Let yourself be surprised for better or for worse, because just like the people from your fav dating app, these colors will likely look nothing like they did on the screen. Test your samples in the brightest and darkest parts of the room, both in natural light throughout the day and in artificial lighting. Did that flirty pink become Barney purple? Maybe that's a problem for you. When we were picking out shades of creamy white for our camper, Rosie (see "So, You Want to Renovate a Vintage Camper?" on page 155), the mixed light made the process of picking a white incredibly hard, and, like, that's already a "kill me" color to decide on. We had to do multiple rounds of sample testing to find one we both loved.

After you've established that you love a color on your wall in both natural light and in the glow of your lamps at night, it's time to take a deep breath and get to painting. If you've got no experience in painting a room, we've got a little guide for you on page 87.

The Right Shade: Furniture

If you're someone who's risk averse, buying a large piece of furniture like a sofa in anything other than a neutral shade may seem like a Big Stupid Bad Decision. And it kind of is! If you grow tired of the color, that pink velvet sofa you bought may make you want to cry. Conveniently, a pink velvet sofa does sound like a very fashionable and appropriate spot to sob in a prom night kind of way. If you eventually decide to change your wall color or your rug, a colorful piece of furniture may clash and limit your options for decorating. So, cheers to you Neutral Sofa People, we totally understand!

On the other hand, a piece of furniture done in a bold statement color can be the sparkling star that *makes* a room. It can be the focal point, almost sculptural in its bold contrast to its surroundings. If it's one of many colorful elements in a room, it can lend a boho eclectic vibe that can feel energizing and inspiring. In one of our most recent living spaces, we had very little going on color wise. The floor plan was completely open, so we kept the walls white, meaning the living space was just white walls and windows. We took a risk and opted for a mustard yellow sofa and blush coffee table to bring color into the space. With a few plants thrown into the mix it all came together for a cozy and colorful room that could so easily have been drab and devoid of personality. All of this to say, hey friend, don't totally write off bold furniture if it's something your eye is often drawn to.

Regardless of which direction you go with furniture, whether it's a soft neutral or something super saturated, remember that all of your primary furniture pieces—sofas, chairs, beds—get dressed up or down with throws and pillows, which may be your chance to bring in contrast.

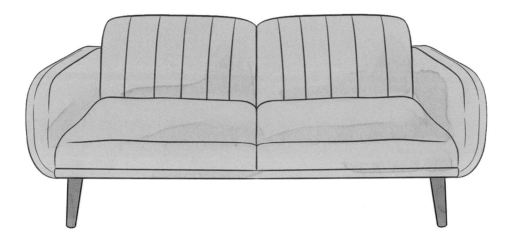

The Right Shade: Finishing Touches

Art, mirrors, statuettes, clocks, window treatments, area rugs, accent rugs, pillows, lamps, vases, candles! Decorative pieces are your chance to really fill in the gaps in a space, and that includes in the color palette.

Unlike walls and furniture, these finishing touches are more or less easy to change and can be done on a tight budget (especially when you can create custom decorative items yourself via DIY!), so don't get too hung up on making it perfect. Let yourself play, do some stretches, move stuff around, and experiment until you find what you like. And if you're looking for a guide to styling all these items, check out page 69.

HOARDING TREASURE

We've never lived anywhere with lots of storage space, but it hasn't kept us from collecting decorative accents we love, even if we don't have the exact right place to put them. We found a pair of vintage tropical bird prints in bamboo frames that we absolutely adored for, like, twenty-five dollars on consignment, and we bought them with the intention to just hold on to them until they had the perfect place in our home or in a future home. That's the beauty of decor that you feel emotionally drawn to: it's the one thing that's totally cool to hoard, particularly for vintage, custom, or handmade pieces that don't depreciate in value the same way big-box retailers' products can.

CHAPTER 6

Designating Space

Pretty much every new construction or recent renovation these days has an open floor plan, where the kitchen, dining, and living areas are all open to one another. The people have spoken, and they have said, "Let there be no walls." It's kind of nice! The vibe is airy, there's a certain freedom to it, but it can also be a bit . . . overwhelming? Like, how do I fill this big void where a home should be in a way that makes sense and also looks good? Can a dining table go in the middle of a room even if the living room is just a few unobstructed steps away? Is it weird for a couch to be right in front of a window? How, dear reader, do we cope with this modern-day conundrum?

Well, we designate space. And while this is a more crucial need for open-floor-plan layouts, spaces of all shapes and sizes can benefit from a little spatial designation and zoning. We're giving you the full guide to designating space and why you should look at an open floor plan as a blank canvas waiting for your strokes of genius, rather than an excuse to sit in the middle of the room and stress-eat takeout (but no shame, and if you tack on some garlic knots, we'll be right over).

Once we know roughly what goes where (the dining table in this corner, the sitting area over here, etc.), we decorate the space to help reinforce that designation. There are three main angles you'll want to approach your decorating from to help designate separate spaces in an open floor plan. Think of these as three avenues you can take to distinguish sections of a larger space.

Over, Under, and Around

Framing a space with a **PENDANT** or **CHANDELIER** *over* it, a rug *under* it, and art or paint or decor *around* it are all ways to help designate an area. Using one, two, or all three of these approaches to set off sections of a larger space, you can design cozy moments even in the most wide-open spaces.

A dining table in an open floor plan can look like it's floating in the void, but add a rug and a chandelier? Boom, looks like it was meant to be there all along. A bar cart by the living space can look like it's randomly placed. But add an oversized framed vintage photo print, a painted mural, or flank it with two big palms? Now it looks like the perfect spot to stir your martinis.

You can use these approaches whether you're working in a 600-square-foot (183 sq m) studio or a 3,000-square-foot (914 sq m) McMansion with an open update. Let's get to it.

Over

A light fixture hanging over an area of your home can serve to highlight and frame the objects below it as a distinct zone. We're firm believers in picking your light fixtures with the same level of intention you'd give to picking art and other decor. For a lot of folks, lighting can be an afterthought, or something seen as more of a utility than an aesthetic choice. But when you add a beautiful, interesting chandelier or pendant to a room, the whole space changes with it. Not to mention, it's the lowest effort ceiling change you can make. If there's no **JUNCTION BOX** in the exact spot you'd like to hang your light fixture, you can always string up a lightweight hanging pendant (such as one with a basket shade) and run the cord down the side of the wall to an outlet. We shed some light (sorry) on how to switch out light fixtures on pages 144–147!

Under

Rugs. This millennia-old woven-fabric art form is the modern answer to all of us, the collective human community, who've decided that carpet is weird and gross, but hard flooring is a little uncomfy and cold. So, we get rugs! They can help bring color and texture and pattern to a space, soften up a room, or hide flooring you can't stand but can't change, and they can tag along with you to every new place you call home. Perhaps most importantly, rugs help build distinct zones. They say, "Here I am, world, a place for things like a sofa or a table." They create borders and boundaries in floor plans where there were none. And they do it oh so well, by just lying there on the floor. What a life.

On the list of design things that we've seen cause panic attacks, choosing a rug falls just below selecting a paint color and just above picking a sofa. So, if you need some guidance, flip back to pages 47–49 for our breakdown of rug sizes, shapes, and styles.

Around

Here's where things get really fun! The *around* realm is where you're going to have the most varied ability and wide scope to designate your space and make it truly unique. Let's talk options!

Paint to Designate Space

The hotly debated accent wall! When you think of "accent walls" you usually picture an entire singular wall being painted a solid color. What we're suggesting here is maybe more accurately called a wall accent—shapes, patterns, or other designs painted onto one wall or spanning multiple walls. We, personally, don't really do single, full accent walls, which isn't to say you shouldn't, just that we don't. Full accent walls can sometimes make a room feel off-balance, and if the intent is to add color to a room, they may actually just add so much contrast with the remaining walls that the rest of the room looks even more color-less. That being said, if a painted *wall accent* is acting as the backdrop to a gorgeous home bar, a dining area, or a desk, it can help ground these items and designate the area as a distinct zone. In a recent apartment, we sectioned off the work area with a painted "rainbow" arch in our favorite hues directly over the desk. It made our workspace—which was right next to our sofa—feel less randomly placed, and also brought a bit of joy to the hours spent sitting there toiling away under the pressures of unchecked capitalism. In one of our friends'

homes, a small corner of the living room has a bright yellow square wall accent that designates it as a play area for her daughter. Visually, it adds a fun pop of color to the space, while also creating a clear boundary for where the toys belong, avoiding clutter throughout the rest of the room. We've got more on how to paint and inspiration for interesting ways to use your new fave paint color on page 87.

Art and Wall Decor to Designate Space

Whether it's a curated gallery wall of mixed art and wall decor, or one larger piece you just love, dressing up the wall around a bar cart, desk, dining table, or sitting area is an effective way to make that space distinct. Beyond canvas and framed print art, there are plenty of items to dress up a wall. Think along the lines of framed memorabilia, woven baskets, and tapestries. The chapter "Creating Personal Pieces for Your Home" (page 135) can help further guide you here.

If you do go the gallery wall route, the driving force behind the selection of wall decor should generally be one of three things: You can make sure all of the art is stylistically similar (order!), make sure everything is stylistically completely different (whimsy!), or find some other similarity beyond style that ties the collection of wall art together, such as a dominant color or subject matter (eclectic!). Whichever route you go—and it is totally up to you sweet friend—make sure it's intentional. It should be easy to read the story of this wall.

Plants to Designate Space

Plants aren't the answer to everything but they're pretty freakin' close, and they just might be your most affordable and exciting option when it comes to designating distinct moments around your home. Tall houseplants with wide canopies (like bird-of-paradise, majestic palms, and some ficus) can perfectly frame a space by setting it apart. Plants with dangly bits do wonders for designating a space when they're hanging down from the ceiling or placed on floating shelves on the perimeter of an area. Just make sure you're taking into consideration each plant's light and water requirements, which pages 128–131 can help you with.

BRING IT BACK TO 2-D

When styling a wall with several pieces of decor, it's not uncommon to be like, "What the shit is happening! This looks all wrong." Use your phone to take a quick pic, step away from the work-space, and analyze how it looks on your two-dimensional screen. From there, make any tweaks or edits that you may catch, and repeat until it looks and feels right on-screen. All this does is offer a different perspective that may help you reimagine the project and fine-tune your gorgeous space.

CHAPTER 7

Finishing Touches to Make It *Chef's Kiss*

Here's the real secret; are you ready? You can make pretty much any blah piece of furniture look "all dressed up with nowhere to be" with a few styling know-hows. Back in our college days we'd scour Craigslist for cheap or free "haul away" furniture. After wading through listings for broken plastic shelving units and honestly somewhat tempting "modeling gigs for cash," we'd find a piece that looked promising, if it could just be styled to perfection—after being drowned in Lysol and blessed by a priest, of course.

But even if you're not in that same desperate boat as we once were, the lesson still stands: The small details of bowls, plants, art, books, statuettes, and other tchotchkes that can be scattered about or organized into beautiful vignettes will round out a space and bring in extra life and personality. You can massively upgrade or complete the look of any piece of furniture with proper and intentional styling. The purpose of these finishing touches is to make a place feel like it's a home that a human with emotions and passions lives in. We're not talking symmetry, but balance. We're not talking perfection, but intention. We're talking building a collection of items that represents you and your taste and finishes off the mood of the room—just like lighting a candle or putting on your favorite album would. And the more *bleh* you feel about your furniture, the more important these finishing touches become.

Creating Vignettes

The very technical definition of a vignette is a mishmash of pieces (art, candles, statuettes, plants, ceramics, etc.) that come together to tell a cohesive story. They're a place to show personality, explore your creative side, and call attention to things you love. You can make a vignette literally anywhere, like on a chest of drawers, credenza, media stand, nightstand, or shelving. And, hey, if designing an entire room feels overwhelming, starting small with something like a vignette may help give you direction for the rest of the space as you work your way outward—because a whole room is really just one large vignette.

INSERT YOURSELF

Is your favorite color missing from the room's furniture and decor? Try finding a piece with that color for your vignette. Does the room lack whimsy or quirk? Take a trip down the weirder aisles of eBay for something with a bit of character. Make sure these pieces are ones that resonate with you and your interests.

How to start making a hodgepodge of favorite items make sense? Well, first acknowledge that the stakes here are incredibly low, so breathe. Then check out our three different methods:

Method 1: Gather and Arrange

Gather all of the items you could possibly imagine using in your vignette and throw 'em on the surface you're styling. Every last thing you could possibly want. Then remove the things that don't make sense for the vignette that should naturally begin forming. This method of chipping away can often be much more efficient than building from a blank slate because you maximize your ability to see the objects interact. Then just boot the ones who aren't vibing with the rest. It's like you're the team captain picking teams in phys ed, but instead of adding new people you're just telling some of them to leave (which somehow sounds sadder than getting picked last).

Method 2: Go Organic

The very basic end goal of a vignette is for your collection of items to look like it organically came together, as if it could've naturally formed that way all on its own. Let's draw on inspiration from your surroundings here, like tree canopies or skylines—there's a wide variety of shapes and heights but only the occasional building or branch stands out, whether it's the tallest, or most brightly colored, the most shocking, or seemingly out of place. Our organic vignette method can be represented by a template we've provided for you on the next page, but as always don't feel like it needs to be followed exactly.

GET A LITTLE WEIRD

Starting from scratch or with very few items? Most of our favorite decorative items come from flea markets, consignment shops, and estate sales. Even if you like to go neutral with your walls and furnishing, we really encourage you to shop for out-of-the-ordinary decorative pieces for styling, such as vintage encyclopedia sets, works of art by relatively unknown artists from flea markets or secondhand stores, or uniquely shaped vases. Generic items from big-box stores are fine fillers, but they're not going to add real interest to a space or be conversation starters. Consider making your own decorative pieces; head to page 135 for inspiration and DIYs!

- Something tallest
- Something widest
- Something much smaller than the rest
- Something symmetrical
- Something asymmetrical
- Something in a color that contrasts with other items as well as with the room

Method 3: The Main Character Method

You know how in every YA fantasy/dystopian movie the fate of the world seems to revolve around one conveniently capable teenager (played by a disturbingly hot adult actor)? That's obviously not how things work in the real world, but we ego-fueled humans find it a formula that's particularly pleasing to us. So, we can borrow from that storytelling trope and approach design from a similar headspace. Start with your favorite object, the one that you want highlighted—your Chosen One—and surround it with things that don't threaten to take attention away from it but support it. Something slightly paler in color, something conceptually related, something that clashes intentionally against it, and a thing or two that draws little attention to itself at all but rounds out the scene, like a background extra.

All three of these methods will require editing, so a few additional words of guidance: Start from the physically largest object and work down to the smallest. Pick your framing piece that designates a vignette's boundaries—for us this is usually artwork or a mirror leaned against the wall. Then work your way down, subtracting things that either you aren't in love with or don't serve a purpose. If you have two or more items that are the exact same height or color or texture, pick just one to keep. The smallest items should go to the front and (usually) to the left or right edge of your vignette. Once you've edited down to your final items, play around with the precise location of each thing. Remember, there is no exact science! Don't stress over it!

Oh, you want some space-specific tips? Thought you might . . .

Styling an Entryway

We try to stay away from words like "energy" and "manifest," but, well, you really gotta consider what kind of energy you want to manifest when you and any guests walk in or out of your front door. A cluttered entryway can quickly scream, "I'm spiraling, my life is out of control!" So, take a moment to consider what you *do* want to see and feel when you walk into the house, as well as what items would make leaving and coming home more convenient. We recommend you have a console table, side table, or shelf, ideally containing a tray that can hold a catch-all for your keys and pocket change, a decorative item (or multiple decorative items as a vignette) to make it feel intentionally styled, and if there's enough light maybe even a plant friend that will greet you upon arrival. If you live somewhere without a clear "entryway," check out our method for designating space on page 69.

Styling Bookshelves

When it comes to styling a bookshelf, the intention is twofold. For starters, you want to create something that aesthetically fits the room and feels like a part of the decor. But also, you'll want to honor your favorite books and create a space that you and your visitors can peruse and get excited about. There are basically two camps of bookshelf-styling theory: curate or crowd.

We like to curate, and recommend you approach bookshelf styling with structure in mind. A shelf literally full of books is the other popular styling preference here, but we find it easier to highlight our favorites when we leave a little space on our shelves. This is not to say less books is better! If you have more books than you can keep track of, you can dedicate one or two shelves at the bottom of a bookcase for more functional storage and then choose which books you'd like to shine more of a spotlight on for the remainder of the shelves closer to eye level and above. Visually, we like to have our shelves become sparser the higher they go, with the very top shelf being mostly decorative items or our most cherished books.

You're basically creating your own personal library that you can organize how you like, Dewey Decimal be damned. You can choose to group books together by categories like "Books We Hated," "Gay Stuff," "Books with Pretty Bindings," "Problematic Faves," "Cooking," and "Books by Friends," or any other, more normal, categories. If it fits your aesthetic and you have enough books to do so, you could also consider coordinating your groups by color to create fun pops of different hues across a shelving unit.

Styling a Coffee Table

An extremely easy formula for you: two or three large, gorgeous books that take up 30 percent of your coffee table space. Next to the books, a tray the same shape as the tabletop, ideally taking up another 30 percent of the space. Within that tray goes a candle of your favorite scent, a saucer with matches or a cute lighter for said candle, and a small and sturdy plant such as a cactus or succulent. The tray is for any loose objects (like a remote) that might otherwise get scattered about and appear messy, the books help set the mood of the room, and the candle is for creating all the good smells. This is like the no-fail formula of coffee table styling, but it's an equation that can of course withstand some addition or subtraction as needed.

Psst: you'd never know it, but we made this coffee table ourselves with some PVC pipes, a wooden top, and black lime-wash paint. We love a budget-friendly DIY, and that's what the entire next section of this book is about! You can find out how we did this coffee table project on probablythis.com.

Styling a Bar Cart

Display the bartending tools you use most and try to incorporate a variety of bottle shapes—we prefer to keep the top shelf sparser, reserving it for a few of our nicer or prettier bottles, attractive glassware, and decorative pieces, while the bottom shelf gets used as a place for storing everything else. Go check out page 211 for help stocking your bar!

Styling a Kitchen Island

The kitchen island is not just for food prep! Any big flat surface in your home can and should be styled. Our advice? Keep your kitchen island styled simply and with more usable objects than not. A bowl of fresh citrus, flowers, greenery in a contrasting vase, or maybe a thoughtfully cute pair of salt and pepper shakers can go a long way toward saying "I'm a very happy and successful homemaker, thank you very much." Place any or all of the above in a shallow tray to ground it and designate it as a decorative space (also making it convenient for moving whenever you need to prepare food or clean the surface).

Styling Your Nightstand

There was a weird phase of our lives early on in our relationship wherein our nightstands would occasionally get overrun with water glasses from previous nights, so, like, baseline don't do *that*. This is not the place for clutter, and we really recommend picking out just one piece of décor, such as a piece of artwork you love or a favorite plant; a lamp; and one or two practical items like a sleep mask and maybe whatever book you're reading at the moment.

THE TAKEAWAY

As far as we see it, styling and vignettes are like the molecules of home design, small pieces that come together to create a whole. Since our entire approach to design has admittedly been fueled by and filtered through social media and our ability to capture design moments with photography, we often think of each room as a series of small and specific vignettes that complement each other in interesting and unexpected ways. Point being, if you can arrange items in a pretty way on a table, you can work your way outwards to designing a whole home.

Small Makers and Businesses We Love to Use in Our Styling

Art Prints and Wall Decor

Bran Sólo
bransolo.com

Broobs
broobs.online

Chris Kelly
etsy.com/shop/
PaintingsByChrisK

Cubs the Poet
cubsthepoet.com

Jan Skacelik
janskacelik.art

JP Brammer/ Hola Papi Shop
holapapishop.com

Logan Ledford
loganledford.com

Oliver Payeur
olivox.com

Rayo & Honey
rayoandhoney.com

Tactile Matter
tactilematter.com

Wit & Delight
witanddelight.com

Ceramics

Ayumi Horie
ayumihorie.com

CBeCeramics
cbeceramics.com

Pansy Ass Ceramics
pansyassceramics.com

Pottery by Osa
potterybyosa.com

Powder Studio Porcelain
powder-studio.com

Sienna Studios
siennastudios.co

Victory Pottery
victorypottery.com

Candles

Boy Smells
boysmells.com

Hazeltine Scent Co.
hazeltinescent.co

Lighting

Gantri
gantri.com

Sazerac Stitches
sazeracstitches.com

Pillows, Rugs, Miscellaneous Decor

Divine Savages
divinesavages.com

Jungalow
jungalow.com

MakeLike
makelike.com

Tamar Mogendorff
tamarmogendorff.com

Vintage and Antique (Furniture and Decor)

Domestica
chairish.com/shop/
domestica

The Lam Label
thelamlabel.com

Object Biographies
objectbio.net

Swoon Rugs
swoonrugs.com

PART 2

DIY

In case we haven't said it enough, we are *always* looking for the cheapest option to make our bizarre ideas come to life, and we're also *always* diving headfirst into things with a blind confidence that we'll figure it out once we're in the thick of it. Enter: DIY. It's incredible what you can do and create with your own hands, the right tools, and the reassurance that if you mess something up, it's okay to just start over. People often ask us, "How do you know how to do *everything*?" and the answer is we, uh, really don't—we're just always willing to teach ourselves and learn by doing, and that's a mindset anyone can be capable of.

CHAPTER 8

Do It Your Dang Self!
An Intro to DIY

We got into DIY projects because we'd never been able to afford hiring out or purchasing all the things we wanted. We promise we'd rather spend our time drinking martinis poolside than, like, researching the best kind of wood to use for the faux stone coffee table we're building (Baltic birch plywood, by the way).

But, sure, there is something to be said about the rewarding feeling of building something yourself, and at the very least the ability to *tell* other people that you built something yourself. It's, like, one of the only socially acceptable things to brag about. Not to mention, when you do build a thing yourself, you can completely customize it to your life. Even when following structured DIYs like the ones we provide in this section, we encourage you to adapt them to your exact desires, needs, and tastes.

On the next page we've got a starting-point checklist for the tools we use most often in our DIY projects. We've sorted our checklist into two levels, the first being more affordable

items we find ourselves using on a regular basis; the second being somewhat more expensive items to keep on your radar for whenever you're ready to dive fully into your DIY fantasy. We built our collection of tools over time, and we tend to avoid buying any super specialized pieces that won't get regular use—sometimes relying on asking around in our friend group or neighborhood Facebook group to see if anyone has one to borrow. That being said, if the options are to buy a tool new or to rent one from the home improvement store, renting can often be almost as expensive as just buying one, which is like, yet another chilling byproduct of capitalism, so it may make sense to just bite the bullet and make the purchase.

Our DIY Newbie Tools and Materials Checklist

Level 1

- [ ] **Cordless drill/driver:** This is likely any DIYer's most used tool and makes a great first purchase for your tool collection. You don't need to drop big bucks here, but keep in mind a good drill can last many years and countless projects, so it's a worthwhile investment.

- [ ] **Drill/driver bit starter set:** Most drill and driver bits are universal for newer tools, meaning they can be used across brands and with either power drills or electric screwdrivers.

- [ ] **Safety gear:** goggles, gloves, ear protectors

- [ ] **Ratchet screwdriver:** This is a handheld screwdriver that allows for interchangeable bits; most work with driver bits from a standard starter set.

- [ ] **Hammer**

- [ ] **Hand saw:** There are many types of hand saws, such as a **HACKSAW**, **BOW SAW**, or **PRUNING SAW**. A hand saw is a great starting point for beginner DIYers, because it allows you to cut wood, PVC, and metal pieces without jumping to the more advanced power saws sooner than you're comfortable with.

- [ ] **Clamps**

- [ ] **Caulk gun**

- [ ] **Sanding blocks**

- [ ] **Tape measure:** We keep a small one in the car for when we're out shopping for furniture and decor, and keep another two at home for when we inevitably are each working on our own projects. Always have one handy!

- [ ] **Spirit level:** This small level is great for making sure whatever you're hanging or building is level, and we often use it during projects to continually make sure everything is correct.

- [ ] **Wood glue**

- [ ] **Paint brush:** Familiarize yourself with the right type and size of brush for each job (keeping in mind what type of paint you will work with). A good brush is meant to last if you properly clean it after each use.

- [ ] **Paint roller and roller head**

- [ ] **Paint roller tray and disposable liners**

- [ ] **Painter's drop cloth or plastic sheeting**

- [ ] **Terry cloth rags**

- [ ] **Putty knife**

Level 2

☐ **Circle saw:** This is a great first power-saw purchase, and it's a saw we use in many of our projects that require we make good, level cuts. You can purchase different blades for different materials (like metal or wood), making it a versatile piece to have in your collection.

☐ **Miter saw:** These bad boys are incredibly useful for making precisely measured angled cuts, also known as **MITER CUTS**. A must-have for projects that have corner joints, like DIY picture frames or anything where a **BUTT JOINT** would be an eyesore.

☐ **Jigsaw:** A jigsaw can be used for cutting freehand, detailed curves and shapes in wood, and other materials when less agile tools can't provide a precise cut.

☐ **Brad nailer or finish nailer:** These nailers are great for DIY projects where you need to do a lot of nailing very quickly. Brad nailers use smaller, thinner 18-gauge nails and are good for decorative projects like paneling or decorative molding, or even small craft projects like birdhouses. Finish nailers use slightly thicker 15- or 16-gauge nails for projects like cabinets, casing, flooring, and baseboards.

☐ **Orbital sander:** This sander is a small, lightweight round sander that is great for smaller jobs or final passes.

☐ **Belt sander:** This sander is a bit more heavy-duty than an orbital sander and is great for stripping and sanding large surfaces like tabletops, counters, and some furniture pieces.

☐ **Worktable or sawhorse:** A quality (and sturdy!) worktable or sawhorse will help ensure your projects are done safely and accurately.

CHAPTER 9

Painting 101

Hooray! You made it through the psychological warfare of choosing a paint color mostly unscathed (see pages 52–56). But now you have to figure out what to do with it. Your options are aplenty and go well beyond just wall-to-wall color! If you've never painted before, we're going to walk you through the process step-by-step, from types of paint to buy to the pure bliss of peeling up the painter's tape after a day of painting.

Types of Paint: How and What to Buy

Paint brands make so many different lines of paint, with different materials and finishes, it can be difficult to parse out what *you* need. So we're breaking that down, in the simplest terms we can manage.

Primer

Primer preps your space to be painted, and *most of the time* is used on new surfaces that have never been painted before—drywall, bare wood, that kind of thing. If your room is already painted one solid, light color, you can

probably skip the step of priming, especially if you opt for multiple coats of a paint-and-primer combo.

Instances where you need to prime prior to painting:

- when you're painting a never-before-painted surface such as new drywall (including a drywall patch after wall damage) or bare wood;

- when you're painting one new color over multiple old colors or textures in the same room or space;

- when you're painting a light color over a much darker color;

- when you're painting latex paint over oil-based paint (oil-based paint may have been used in an older home and is especially common on trim and older cabinetry)—you'll need to prepare the surface with a light sanding, **TRISODIUM PHOSPHATE** treatment (a cleaner that will promote adhesion), and priming. If you're tackling that specific scenario, we recommend doing a little bit more research on the topic before getting started.

Primer can actually come in many shades, not just the stark white color so often associated with it. Tinted primer is a good option for darker paint colors, so that your paint doesn't have to work against a bright white behind it, like it would with untinted primer. Ask a store associate which primer they recommend for your color. Hot tip here: Shopping in paint stores (as opposed to general home-improvement stores) is a smart move if you're not exactly sure what you need or are new to painting—you'll typically have associates with professional knowledge who can help guide your decision making. A *lot* of what we've learned has been taught to us by Sherwin-Williams store associates.

Paint

The most common type of paint used in homes is latex or acrylic-latex paint. It's probably what's on the walls surrounding you right now! Latex paint comes in several different finishes and is your go-to for your walls. It's water-based, which makes for easy application and clean-up (just rinse brushes with water and wipe up any spills or splatters as they happen!) For the sake of keeping all of our lives simple, latex paint is what you should stick to for most home projects.

LIME PAINT

Yes, we said we'd keep things simple, but we're liars, and there's one more type of paint we want to tell you about! Lime paint (also called limewash or limestone paint) is a specialty paint, available in a variety of colors, that has limestone mineral in it and can be used to create a plaster effect on walls. It's what's in the room on the cover of this book and can also be seen on page 22. We love how much character it adds for very little effort, and it can be styled in plenty of different ways, from ultra-modern to baroque or even tropical. Specialty brands like Color Atelier sell it by the quart or gallon for prices comparable to higher-end traditional latex paints, and applying it is pretty simple!

Finishes

Picking a paint finish is actually super important and something we really should all be talking about more! Once you've settled on a color, you'll need to select from a range of four or five finishes, from **MATTE** (not shiny) to **GLOSS** (very shiny)—with options like **SATIN** and **SEMI-GLOSS** in between. Some brands offer different levels of sheen with cute names like "**EGGSHELL**" or "**PEARL**," so you'll want to check the scale of whatever brand you're using to be fully informed. The higher the gloss, the easier it is to wipe down and clean, and glossier paints will scuff less easily. Matte finishes show fewer of the wall's textural imperfections because they reflect less light, but they can be really tough to clean and any marks will likely require touch-ups. Whenever we go with a matte finish, we keep a quart of that color on hand to paint over any small marks or scuffs that happen over time.

So, when it comes to selecting a finish, consider where in your home the paint will go, but also which finish you find most aesthetically pleasing. Areas that are not high-traffic or are not prone to spills (living rooms, offices, and bedrooms) are the places that are most safe for matte finishes. Rooms that get beat up and require more regular cleaning (kitchens and bathrooms and, sure, bedrooms if you're adventurous) are where you typically want to use a glossier finish. But like we mentioned, finish is important for both function and aesthetic. A quality paint in a high-gloss finish will have an extremely shiny, glass-like appearance that can bring a splash of drama even with neutral paint colors. Bold colors in a glossier finish may overwhelm a space, but using a matte finish can help subdue the color's intensity, making for a better fit.

Quality and Quantity

Most paint brands have tiers of quality, with some lower-end paints running around thirty dollars per gallon and higher-end paints around a hundred dollars per gallon. High-quality paint is really, really nice to work with; it'll adhere better, have a more saturated pigmentation, and provide more coverage. However, if you're on a tight budget and, say, a renter who will need to return your walls back to the previous color before moving out in a year, cheap paint will do the trick!

As for quantity, assuming you're using a paint-and-primer, you'll need 1 gallon (3.8 liters) per coat on 400 square feet (122 square meters) of coverage area, and we pretty much always recommend doing two coats. Add the lengths of all the walls to find the total perimeter, and multiply that perimeter by the ceiling height—this is your wall square footage. To be even more exact, multiply the width of each window or door by its height; then add those together and subtract *that* number from your total wall square footage to find the true number of square feet you're going to need to cover. There are also plenty of online calculators to help you calculate the precise amount of paint you need to buy. In general, for any room larger than a small bathroom or closet, you're going to need more than 1 gallon (3.8 liters) of paint.

An Example (Math!)

Wall 1:	10ft	Window 1:	4ft × 6ft = 24ft^2
Wall 2:	14ft	Window 2:	4ft × 6ft = 24ft^2
Wall 3:	10ft	+ Door:	3ft × 8ft = 24ft^2
Wall 4:	14ft		

Total (perimeter):	48ft		72ft^2
	× 10ft (ceiling height)		

480 ft^2

480 ft^2 − 72 ft^2 = 408 ft^2

So, for a room of this size, covering 400 feet^2 per gallon (122 m^2 per 3.8 liters), and at two coats, you'll need about 2 gallons (7.6 liters) of paint!

THE TAKEAWAY

That was a lot of info, sorry. In case your eyes glazed over and you missed it all, here's the TLDR: for painting an average room in your home, you're going to want to grab a couple gallons of a latex paint-and-primer in a finish that will both fit your desired aesthetic and protect your walls—lower gloss for rooms like an office or living room and a glossier finish for rooms like a kitchen or bathroom.

How to Paint

If the room you're about to bless with a fresh coat of paint is full of furniture, either move it to the center and cover, or remove it from the room entirely. If possible, open any windows to create air circulation and ventilation because your precious little lungs don't need a chemical treatment.

You'll need:

Paint (see pages 88–91 to determine which paint and the quantity you'll need)

60-yard (55 m) roll of multi-surface painter's tape (we recommend FROG TAPE)

Painter's drop cloth or heavy plastic sheeting (word of warning: Canvas drop cloths alone won't block big spills from seeping through to the floor beneath, so practice caution and wipe spills as soon as they happen!)

A 2-inch (5 cm) trim brush in a material compatible with your paint type

A paint roller (you may want one that has an extendable arm, if you have high ceilings) and tray

Paint roller heads in a material compatible with your paint type. Choose a NAP that is right for your surface. Rougher surfaces like brick need thicker naps that can get into cracks and crevices (up to ¾"/2 cm) while flat untextured walls will need just ¼".

1   Wipe down your baseboards, even if they look clean! Dust and other gross crap can prevent your painter's tape from totally adhering to your wall, which can leave room for paint to leak into cracks where the tape doesn't fully make contact with the wall.

2   Lay your painter's cloth on the ground and apply the tape to the baseboards, or if there are no baseboards, apply it to the corner between the wall and the floor. Make sure you smooth the tape down firmly so that it's adhering to any bumps or irregularities on the surface. We want this to be Fort Knox level sealed so that we can drink our martinis and paint our trim without concern.

3   Start with your edging brush and paint a 2- to 3-inch-thick (5 to 7.5 cm) trim along the ceiling, door, and window **CASING**, and floor or baseboards. Don't apply too much pressure here as we don't want to force any of our paint under the clean line we created with the tape.

4   Roll the roller into your tray's basin to coat on all sides (when putting a dry roller head into your paint tray for the first time, roll it back and forth seven or eight times to make sure the paint has fully saturated the material) then gently roll it along the ridges of the pan to remove the excess. Use your roller to fill in the wall, working in a V or N shape to apply the paint, knocking out a section of about 10 square feet (25 square meters) before rolling it back in the paint

Continues

tray. We're looking for a light, even coat here—loading on the paint or applying a lot of pressure on the roller might be faster, but it's also going to cause an uneven application, and a higher chance of mess. Continue until your wall is covered.

5   Let the paint dry for at least 2 hours before applying a second coat (check product instructions for exact times as it does vary). About an hour after applying your final coat, remove the painter's tape by gently pulling it back on itself. Removing it at an angle or by pulling too hard may result in the tape removing part of the new paint job, which will make you scream.

Accents, Murals, Patterns, and Shapes

Your options for painting go beyond just: "I'm painting my room blue!" As mentioned in the chapter "Designating Space" on page 61, paint is an effective way to set off smaller areas in a room, using accents, shapes, and murals to frame a bed or desk or other piece of furniture against a wall.

For something that's a bit more timeless than geometric accents, consider painting just the bottom half of a room. If you look at popular designs from the sixties, and even back to some Victorian-era homes, you'll come across rooms that have wall color from the **BASEBOARD** to just about 40 inches (about 100 cm) high. Most often in older designs this would be painted **PANELING** such as **WAINSCOTING**, but we can approximate that effect with paint alone by painting up to a certain height along the wall. Just tape off your stopping point using a **LASER LEVEL** to ensure an even line, then paint those half-walls following our "How to Paint" instructional (page 93). As opposed to painting a full room, this method takes less time, money, and effort for a potentially more impactful design choice.

DIY Painted Arches and Circles

One of our favorite cost-effective ways to dress up a space, these little baddies have become quite trendy on the internet in recent years. That's okay though; just because something is a trend doesn't mean it's off-limits! Use painted arches and circles to set apart shelving units, create a "headboard" for your bed, or even for smaller projects like framing the edges of a gallery wall. The only rule is that you'll want your arch or circle to be the width of any piece of furniture it's framing, or wider—any undersized painted shape may look a little awkward.

You'll need:

Measuring tape

String

Scissors

Pencil

Masking tape

Yardstick or 4-foot (1.2 m) level

Paint

Edging brush

Painter's tape

Paint roller and tray

An assistant

1   Decide how wide you'd like your circle or arch to be, then divide that number by 2 to get your radius. Cut a piece of string that same length, plus 3 extra inches (7.5 cm). Tie one end of the string around the pencil and tape the string in place so it can't slide up or down. Stretch the string out next to your tape measure to find that exact radius measurement and use a piece of masking tape to mark that spot. Don't cut off the excess; you'll want to leave a bit of string to hold onto later.

2   Have your assistant hold the loose end of the string in the exact center of where your shape will go. Then, holding the pencil so the string is taut, trace the shape onto the wall. For a full circle, just trace all the way around. For an arch, trace the top half of the circle, then use a yardstick to draw straight lines from the farthest left and right points of the circle down to the baseboard or the floor.

3   For the straight sides of an arch, use painter's tape for a clean line. Carefully paint the curved edges with the edging brush or, if it makes you more comfortable, a small detail brush from an art supply store. Then use the paint roller to fill in the rest of the shape. If there are any visible pencil lines, gently erase them using the pencil's eraser once the paint has dried.

CHAPTER 10

Repairing and Refurbishing Vintage Furniture Pieces

One of our favorite ways to add life to a room is through secondhand finds—it's less rude to the planet and will give your space something truly unique. Refreshing old furniture you already own, buying new-to-you furniture secondhand, and buying outdated pieces with the intention of repurposing them are all budget- and eco-friendly decor solutions. So, if you don't do it, well, we *will* blame you for the climate crisis. In this chapter we've got the basics of what to look for when buying consigned or thrifted pieces, methods for refinishing, restaining, and painting, as well as some tips on when it's truly time to say, "*Ciao, besos!*" to a piece that's worn itself out.

While we're never going to stop you from going full-blown vintage with all your furniture (we did this in one of our past bedrooms!), we typically use vintage pieces in combination with newer pieces to strike the perfect balance of cozy and fresh. This helps make the vintage pieces feel less, well, old and any new pieces feel less like sterile items straight from a catalog.

So, before we get to the physical process of refurbishing, let's talk about where you can find quality secondhand pieces, either in good enough shape to use as-is or in poorer condition for you to spruce up yourself. If you've already got a piece that you'd like to give a refresh to, skip ahead a few pages!

Where to Shop

Consignment Shops

If you're not familiar with consignment shops, think of them like thrift stores' and pawn shops' older, hotter, cooler brother. They're a place where folks can list their secondhand and vintage pieces for sale, and then the profit from the sale is split between the shop and the owner of the item. Every consignment shop works differently, but most have a system where every thirty days the item is in the store (or five weeks, or two months, etc.), it goes down in price—so if you see something you love but it's a bit out of budget, check their policy and the date on the tag to see if a markdown is coming up, or if a markdown already applies. Also, because the shop essentially acts as a middleman between the customer and the consignor (the person who brought the item into the shop), there's often room for negotiating. Prices can range from very cheap to higher end, but consignment stores are our number one go-to and a great place to get your little pinky toes wet in the world of vintage shopping. We've found some of our most cherished pieces on consignment and it's an incredible feeling to fall in love with a cool old piece just waiting for a new home.

Flea Markets

A flea market is a collection of vendors selling secondhand and sometimes handmade items ranging from furniture to clothing to electronics. Some are super curated and amazing while others can be full of junk, but if you're lucky enough to live near a large flea market that has vendors with quality pieces, you better make that one of your first stops when adding decor to your home or doing a redesign. Some flea markets are seasonal, some are year-round, and some have seemingly random hours of operation—your best bet for finding a good one near you is doing a little sleuthing online and visiting any that looks promising. Once you find one you love, you'll become familiar with which vendors carry the good stuff.

Estate Sales

There's no way around saying it: An estate sale means someone died and now all their stuff is

for sale. It's not necessarily the most joyous occasion to shop, but someone does need to buy all that stuff, and anyone who had a nice collection of pieces would be happy to know their items are getting a new home rather than ending up in a landfill. Except us. We would prefer to have all of our items buried with us. Estate sales are kind of a crapshoot, but there are reputable companies that run them, and many will only take on homes with objects of value or that have curated collections. You can often get an online preview of what's in the home before going, and make sure you pay attention to exact times and dates of the sale and get there early because if it's "a good one," every vintage shopper in the area will be there on the hunt.

While you can sometimes find people posting about them on places like Facebook Marketplace, the best resources are estatesales. net and estatesales.org, where you can find information about estate sales near you weeks in advance and see a preview of what's inside. Some even allow you to purchase or put an offer in on items online without ever having to visit the home.

Websites like Chairish and eBay

Online shopping for secondhand pieces is totally a thing! It's not our favorite—usually the best way to assess the quality and condition of a secondhand item is in person—but online shopping is an incredibly efficient way to sift through hundreds of items quickly. Chairish, Etsy, eBay, Facebook Marketplace, and Craigslist can actually get you some really amazing results. If you find the right price on the perfect piece, paying any additional shipping costs might be totally worth it to you.

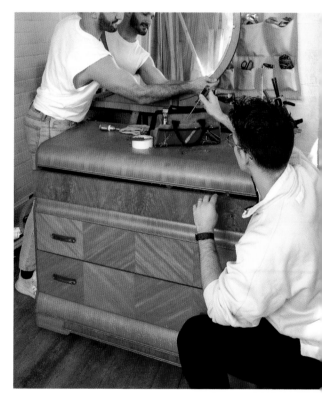

Inspecting and reassembling a vintage waterfall dresser after a quick drawer pull repair job—sometimes even just a little super glue can make a big difference!

What to Look for
When Vintage Shopping

Think of walking into a vintage store or an estate sale like going on a blind date . . . it could go horribly wrong!!! Or you could meet the love of your life. This is what makes vintage shopping such a fun adventure all on its own, and if you do it enough, you'll one day find that forever love. That's what happened when we found our vintage bamboo canopy bed . . . for $125. We had to furnish an entire bedroom from scratch, and once we found that bed we immediately had a direction for the room. We went in with an open mind and left with a fully developed concept, all based around one piece.

Of course, whenever you're shopping used pieces, you'll come across items that look, well, used. We actually don't mind little scrapes and bruises on an old piece of wooden or iron furniture. It adds character, it shows it's been used, and it can quickly cozy up a space and make it feel like it's been lived in and loved for years. That being said, when fabrics are involved, like with sofas or chairs or tufted jewel-toned velvet headboards from 1962 that say, "I'm yours, darling," it's best to use caution. Check fabrics very carefully for wear and tear, ensure there is no musty smell (it may be impossible to get rid of entirely without reupholstering), and give it a good feel to make sure it's not itchy. There's always the option to have a piece you love reupholstered, but that can get expensive very

quickly and can be a pretty adventurous DIY to take on yourself. But hey, maybe you need an adventure, in which case, knock yourself out. The exception to the "be cautious of used fabrics while vintage shopping" rule excludes rugs, which are easy to deep clean and won't be up against your face, like a sofa might be.

Repairing and Refurbishing Old Pieces

Whether it's an item that you've had for years, or something you bought because we just now told you to, there comes a time in a piece of furniture's life when it's going to need a little makeover. Depending on what the item is, what it's made of, and how it'll be used, this can happen a million different ways. On the next few pages, we'll tackle your options for two basic materials even the most unseasoned DIYer can tackle: wood and iron. When there is damage to wood beyond a slight nick, ding, or scratch—say, evidence of pet damage or peeling sealant or paint—it could be time to refinish it.

SIDE NOTE: WE DON'T DO DIY REUPHOLSTERING

In general, this is something we try to avoid, to be honest! Reupholstering is an art unto itself, and while it's totally something that you can take a stab at, a poor-quality reupholstery job can ruin an oh-so-special vintage piece rather than make it shine. It's important to know your limits! For that reason, we always hire this task out to a professional, even though it can be really expensive. If you're purchasing an item from a dealer with the intention of having it reupholstered, ask the seller if they have any recommendations on who to go with.

Take several photos, including details of any damage, and send them to multiple reupholsterers in your area to get quotes before buying the piece so you can assess its true cost (of course, if you're in a higher-stakes setting like a crowded flea market or auction, there may be no time to wait for replies). Keep in mind that with something like reupholstery, you often get what you pay for, so if this is a special piece to you or a gorgeous reupholstering job could significantly increase the value, you'll want to go with the best upholsterer you can find.

Staining or Painting Wooden Furniture

Refinishing your wooden furniture is actually very simple if you've got the right tools and follow some DIY basics! Let's walk you through the process before we jump on in. You're basically going to clean off your piece, give it a few sanding passes to remove the previous finish and leave the surface so fresh and so smooth, and then apply your new stain or paint!

But safety first: If you're planning to sand a piece of furniture that has paint on it and there's a chance lead paint is present (especially common with older vintage or heirloom pieces), perform a lead test prior to sanding. You can purchase instant lead tests at most home improvement stores, and if your item tests positive for lead it's best to **WET-SAND** your piece or use a chemical stripper that will avoid the dispersal of lead dust. Whenever working with any piece that has lead paint, you need to wear a respirator designed to filter out lead and follow local guidelines for disposal.

You'll need:

All-purpose cleaner

Terry cloths or rags

Painter's tape

Orbital sander or sanding block

Sandpaper in a range of grits: 80 at the low end to up to 400 max (see Notes)

Stain brush or paint brush

Wood stain or furniture paint (and primer) formulated for wood

Dust mask (or lead respirator, if needed)

1 If the piece you're working on can be dissassembled, do so. Disassembling before painting/staining each individual component is the easiest way to ensure a smooth and even coat over the entire surface without having any excess pool up in hard-to-reach areas like cracks and corners. Thoroughly clean your piece with all-purpose cleaner and a rag to remove any dust or gunk that will get in your way.

2 Remove or tape off any non-wooden components, like hardware, pulls, drawer tracks, or fabrics.

3 Working outdoors or in a very well-ventilated workspace that you don't mind getting messy, sand down your furniture. Starting with your orbital sander (or sanding block) and sandpaper in your lowest grit, work your way around the piece—if using sanding blocks or any "in-line" sanders, make sure you're sanding *with* the grain. You may need to switch to hand sanding for any corners or grooves that your sander can't reach. After a full pass with your **MEDIUM GRIT** sandpaper to remove the majority of the previous stain or paint, use your **FINE GRIT** for a second

pass, and finally give it an ultra-smooth finish with your **VERY FINE GRIT** paper.

4   Once you've sanded, it's time to wipe down again to remove any dust you've created and get to staining or painting. The world of furniture stains and paints is vast and broad and can be overwhelming, but just like with wall paint you can always get a small test size to see how a color looks on your piece before committing to it. If painting, make sure to prime first. For most furniture pieces, a spray primer will be the easiest to apply.

5   Stain or paint your piece according to the instructions on the product you're using. Do multiple thin coats of paint or stain, and avoid globbing it on. If you disassembled your item at the beginning of this project, allow for a full 24-hour dry time before reassembling. Now OMG, look at the cute new piece you restored all by yourself!!

NOTES:

Sandpaper Grit: The lower the grit, the rougher it is—so be careful not to use anything that is so rough that it creates deep scars on your piece. Sandpaper labeled **COARSE** or **EXTRA COARSE** (usually anything lower than 80 grit) is too coarse for furniture. The lowest you'll want to go for this project is **MEDIUM GRIT** (between 80- and 100-grit). **FINE GRIT** (between 120 and 220) is good for your second smoothing pass, and **VERY FINE GRIT** (240 to 400) is good for a finishing pass before painting or staining. In order to guarantee a smooth finish, make sure to increase the grit number gradually—don't go from a medium grit to a very fine grit without using a fine grit between them.

Paint: Standard wall paint isn't a smart option for furniture, which will get plenty of wear and tear. Instead, pick a paint designed for furniture, such as an enamel paint. We typically use a brush for painting our furniture, but if you want the absolute best quality, using a paint sprayer will give you an even and professional finish.

Refurbishing Iron Furniture

If you have a piece of iron furniture like an outdoor chair or antique sewing table that's gone from "charming" old to, like, "no one wants to touch this" old, it's time to give it new life! Compared to wooden furniture, iron furniture can be more tedious to refinish because iron pieces tend to have many more decorative curves and grooves than wood, and because iron is just physically harder to sand, so summon all the patience you've got. Make sure to wear the proper safety gear and do a lead test prior to sanding down any painted surfaces.

You'll need:

Safety goggles, gloves, and dust mask (or **RESPIRATOR**, if needed)

Wire brush

Power drill fitted with a paint and rust-remover-disk power tool bit*

Orbital sander or sanding blocks**

Fine-finishing sandpaper: 100, 150, and 220 grit

Acetone

Terry cloths or work rags

Rust-resistant spray primer

Exterior spray paint in color and finish of your choice

Clear enamel spray paint

1 Working outdoors or in a well-ventilated workspace, lay down your furniture or piece on a clean work surface. Remove any rust with the rust-removing drill bit and the wire brush. You may need to switch back and forth between the two to get the job done.

2 Once the majority of the rust is gone, use your orbital sander, sanding blocks, or single sheets of sandpaper if hand-sanding to sand the surface down. Start with your

NOTES:

***Rust-removing tool bit:** Manufacturers like 3M sell power drill bits that have wire brushes on them meant to warp-speed spin-and-remove rust. Though they sell ones designed for more intricate or grooved surfaces, they'll do best on flat surfaces. If you don't want to go this route, just know that hand-sanding rust off a large piece of furniture is really quite a process but it can be done with 80 grit sandpaper and a lot of patience.

****Using orbital sander and sanding block:** These will come in handy for any flat metal surfaces like the seat of a chair but won't do you much good on very intricate surfaces, like a wrought iron bench. If your surface is intricate, you may need to skip the orbital sander and sanding blocks altogether, instead using your wire rust removal tools and hand-sanding to get the job done.

lowest grit and work your way up to the 220 grit, taking your time to give a thorough pass over the piece with each subsequent grit of sandpaper.

3   Use acetone and your cleaning rags to wipe down the surface, removing dust or impurities.

4   Prime with a rust-resistant spray primer according to the instructions for your primer of choice—for the best finish, multiple light coats are better than a single heavy coat, which could result in drips or an uneven texture.

5   Use a spray paint in the color and finish of your choice to coat your piece. Once the paint has cured (curing times will be on the package), we like to finish with a clear coat of spray enamel to prevent future chips or damage.

We used this method to refurbish the exterior of a clawfoot tub in our home. Make sure to pick appropriate paint types for your iron pieces, such as using an exterior enamel paint for items that will be in wet areas or outdoors.

SANDBLASTING AND POWDER COATING

If you've got a super-intricate and ornate metal piece that needs refurbishing, or just one that you want to have professionally refinished, sandblasting and powder coating are great options.

Sandblasting is the process of, well, blasting an item with sand to remove all the layers of paint and rust for a fresh and smooth return to its original metal.

Powder coating is basically just very fancy spray-painting done by a professional, and any powder coater will first sandblast your item to give their work a fresh and even base. Many of these professionals will also be able to weld any cracks, breaks, or other imperfections. Just do a search for powder coaters near you to find the right person for the job.

Knowing When It's Time to Say Goodbye

With all this talk about how to reuse and repurpose pieces, it feels wrong to not address the fact that, yes, it's okay for you to get rid of things, and, no, it doesn't make you a bad person! If you've outgrown an item you once loved, or if that side table you snagged at an antiques mall years ago just got plowed over by your husky, you've got options.

For items in fair to good condition:
If you're, like, financially stable, consider donating it to any local housing aid or mutual aid programs that support marginalized communities. If you could use the cash, quality vintage pieces can be shopped around to your local antique and decor dealers or consignment shops who may take them on to sell for you, and newer mass-produced pieces (like anything from Pottery Barn) will get snatched up on Facebook Marketplace and Craigslist. You can always list vintage pieces on those websites, too, but their value may not be as appreciated by the wider customer base.

For items in poor condition: List these for free as a "curb alert" in your neighborhood Facebook or NextDoor groups for anyone in your community to take and use for parts or try their hand at fixing up. It's better than having these items end up in a landfill!

CHAPTER 11

Container Gardens: From Indoor Herb Gardens to Raised Beds

Nothing says: "I'm better than you" more loudly than picking fresh mint from your herb garden to muddle into a cocktail or plop into an iced tea. Container gardens for herbs or other edible plants serve a utility while adding charm to your indoor or outdoor space. In this chapter we'll go over the basics of container gardening, including creating an herb garden, building raised beds, and other DIYs to bring life into your home or outdoor area.

Our very first container garden was a mix of small clay pots, each housing a single herb, all placed in the windowsill above our kitchen sink. Basic, yes, but even just this very simple and cheap addition made our then-tragic apartment kitchen feel a little more like a homestead. Over the years we've experimented with different styles of container gardening, ranging from those little clay pots to our current raised beds that are big enough to make any doomsday-prepper feel ready for the apocalypse. From basil to bell peppers, we've tried our hand at growing many of the things we enjoy using in our cooking—and yes, there have been some mass casualty events along the way; it comes with the territory of trying something new in the gardening world. We encourage you to not think about that and dive right in.

Creating an Herb Garden

Containers

You can either plant each herb in its own pot or plant all your herbs in one pot. Each of these has its own perks—individual pots for each plant allow you to more closely control each plant's water and sun and adjust accordingly. Your basil may end up wanting a more hearty watering than your sage, or your mint might flourish closest to the window, where it's too bright for your thyme. On the other end, having all of your herbs planted together in one container can be visually stunning—as long as they're not all dead because you couldn't meet their individual needs! Herbs tell you what they need, drooping when thirsty, yellowing when overwatered, getting shriveled from too much sun, and producing spindly offshoots when they need more sun, so pay attention and adjust accordingly.

Placement

Whether growing indoors or outdoors, you want to put herbs in a spot with four to six hours of sunlight per day, ideally a south- or southwest-facing window (in the Northern Hemisphere) that gets lots of light during peak hours, 10 A.M. to 6 P.M. That being said, one of our most bountiful herb gardens was on a north-facing patio that had no direct light at all, so it's safe to say that sometimes in life everyone is lying to you. A little experimentation might just pay off.

Selecting Your Herbs

We recommend just sticking with herbs you like to cook with. We go through basil upsettingly fast, tossing it by the fistful into pestos and pastas and dressings and sauces. So, we always keep a 2:1 basil-to-everything-else ratio. We also always get a lot of use out of our mint plants, though mint grows so fast that it can be hard to keep up with, and our chive plants give us the happiest platefuls of loaded baked potatoes. Rosemary and thyme are both incredible for roasted vegetables, sauces, and in spice rubs for beef, chicken, or portobello mushrooms. We've done sage and oregano but realized we don't really use those things in our cooking that often, and so they just sort of sat there unused until one day we noticed they had, in fact, perished. So anyway, just plant herbs you actually want to use.

Building Raised Bed Gardens

We've always half-joked about buying a bunch of land and starting a utopian commune—think Smurfs, not Jonestown—and a big part of that would, of course, be bountiful garden beds! Raised garden beds are the pinnacle of domesticity, and a fantastic way to grow your food in a safe and controlled environment. If you live in a home with a backyard that gets even partial light, you too can have a lush, full garden. Building raised garden beds is actually very easy and just requires you do a bit of project planning.

As for cost, not gonna lie, this project can be nearly free or shockingly expensive. We've outlined your options to help you choose what's right for you, and the steps to make it amazing!

Location

Different plants thrive in different conditions, and hopefully that's not news to you, or you may be a lost cause. In order to grow a vegetable garden that makes lots of edible veggies and fruits, you'll need at least six hours of direct light a day. If your spot is shadier, you can still create raised garden beds for some shade-loving ornamentals as well as some vegetables that can tolerate lesser amounts of sun. You can have a luscious garden in most climates, but you've gotta make sure you're planting appropriately for the amount of sunlight your garden will receive each day and for your **HARDINESS ZONE**, a guide to growing based on your geographic location. Find your hardiness zone online (a simple Google search will give you all the info you need!) and then see how much sunlight the different plants in your zone require. Spend a day or two paying close attention to the amount of light your yard gets to make sure you're picking out plants that will thrive in whatever conditions you have.

Size

We chose to make our raised beds about 24 inches (about 60 cm) high after deciding that was the best height for us to gracefully bend over them in photos (and to make tending the garden convenient). You can do raised beds as low as 8 inches (20 cm) to save a bit of time and money, if you have decent ground soil beneath the beds (typically raised beds are bottomless, meaning that anything growing in shallow raised beds will likely reach the soil beneath the bed). As a necessary aside, if you have poor soil quality (say, you live in an area with clay-heavy soil or have reason to believe your ground may contain toxins), you won't want the roots to reach the ground soil. You can use landscaping fabric beneath the bed soil to stop the roots from growing further while still allowing drainage, but that will require you to build your beds high enough to give your plants enough depth to thrive (generally about 18 inches/46 cm, but you should research the rooting depth of specific plants to better plan your beds' dimensions). Also consider ease of access—the beds shouldn't be so wide that you can't access the entire surface of the garden. We found that a 32-inch (about 80 cm) width was comfortable for us to reach all the way across.

Good Wood

You can use plenty of different kinds of lumber for a raised garden bed, but we chose to go with western red cedar because it's naturally rot resistant, looks beautiful, and will last for many years. If you can swing the cost, your best bets are cedar, redwood, or pine. Prioritize local lumberyards over big home-improvement stores; they'll be more knowledgeable and occasionally cheaper. Pressure-treated lumber produced after 2004 is safe to use and likely your cheapest option, though the online organic gardening community tends to get big mad about it, because it's chemically treated. Pressure-treated lumber produced before 2004 isn't considered safe for food-bearing plants, as it may contain harmful levels of arsenic. Don't reuse old wood if you're not sure of its previous use or if it may have been in contact with harmful chemicals. Don't use old railroad ties—they may contain creosote, which is toxic.

To Stain or Not to Stain?

If you want to stain your wood, you'll do so first thing and allow it to dry fully before assembling your raised beds. Staining all sides makes sure the wood is fully protected from moisture and sun, so that you'll have beautiful garden beds for as long as possible. Linseed oil, tung oil, beeswax, and whey are common stain bases that are safe for edible plants. If you don't plan to grow food in your beds, feel free to use traditional deck or wood stain.

TIPS FOR CARE

Mulching beds helps with temperature and moisture regulation, which in turn may help extend your growing season.

Plan your pairings! Pairings like tomato, basil, and onion or corn, beans, and squash are classic combinations that won't compete with each other.

DIY Raised Garden Beds

You'll need:

⁵⁄₄ × 6-inch (3 × 15 cm) lumber cut to size and stained (if doing so)

Square corner posts for each corner, cut to whatever height the beds will be

Landscaping fabric and garden staples (if using— see page 114 for guidance)

Deck screws

Power drill

Landscaping fabric

Miter saw (if making cuts on site)

1 Lay your first layer of planks in place. Drill adjacent side pieces into each corner post and double check that the angles of the side joints are precisely 90 degrees before continuing—it's way easier to fix that now than later.

2 With the first layer of your bed complete, cut landscaping fabric (if using) to the size of the bed and stake or staple it into the ground—it'll block weeds and other root systems from growing up into your beds, stop your plants' roots from growing into the ground soil below, and still allow for proper water drainage. Landscaping fabric isn't necessary if your ground soil is good quality for whatever you're growing and should only be used when your container gardens are tall enough to fully accommodate your plants' root systems.

3 Now get to assembling the remainder of the bed! Rest each plank on top of the plank below it and drill it into the corner post, making your way around the garden bed until it's fully

TIPS TO MAKE THIS AS CHEAP AS POSSIBLE

Use repurposed wood from your own property or local salvage yards, or check online listings for free or cheap lumber listed for local pickup. If going any of these routes, make sure to follow the safety protocols outlined on page 115.

If you are going to buy new wood, our most budget-friendly recommendation is new fence posts. Fence posts will be slightly less sturdy (i.e., don't put your weight on the finished product) and won't last as long but will hold in soil and vegetables just

fine! Six-foot-tall cedar fence posts are our recommendation, as they will look nice and hold up well for several years.

Skip the garden center and call a local bulk topsoil company to see if you can score soil on the cheap. Use a soil tester to make sure you get your soil pH where it needs to be for a successful garden (typically between 6.0 and 7.0, but different species' ideal pH can vary). Be aware that you may need to supplement with compost or other additives to strike the right nutrient balance.

assembled. We kept a miter saw on-site to adjust for any imperfections

4 Optional: Use a miter saw to cut 45-degree angles into your top layer of lumber to create a "lip" for storing pruning shears or gloves or cocktails. The lumber for this lip needs to be approximately 6 inches (15 cm) longer than the corresponding pieces below it to account for the angle cut, so take care when measuring or ordering that you've got enough wood to work with.

5 Fill your bed with the soil blend of your choice (see notes on soil, page 119) and drench with water. Let the soil rest for a few days before planting.

Easy Alternatives: Single-Plank Raised Garden Bed

The above instructions are for garden beds like the ones pictured, multiple planks stacked to a height of about 24 inches (60 cm). You could also just use one plank per side as long as the soil beneath the beds is in decent condition and safe for growing in. If going that route, consider these notes and changes.

- Skip the landscaping fabric, as it will block your plants' roots from growing into the soil beneath the ground.

- Prior to building your beds, till the soil beneath and use a soil test kit to measure for nutrients, pH, and drainage. You can pick up a lab test kit at many garden centers or online for between $20 and $30.

You can also find soil meters for regular use that will monitor pH levels, sunlight, and moisture. Based on your results, you may need to supplement your soil with organic matter and fertilizer to create an optimal growing environment.

- Feel free to skip the corner posts and drill the planks directly into each other or use metal L-brackets.

Miniature "Raised Bed" Gardens

No room for raised beds but love the look? Make them tiny! These miniature raised beds are an adorable addition to an apartment balcony, patio, or other small outdoor space.

You'll need:

Wooden crates (can be found at your local craft store)

Scissors

Burlap

Hot glue gun

1 Cut and fit the burlap to cover the inside of the crate.

2 Hot glue the burlap to the interior perimeter.

3 Cut off any excess around the top.

4 Fill with soil and plants!

NOTE: The burlap will not last long with direct sun or heavy rain exposure, so it is ideal for use on a covered balcony or patio.

Caring for Your Container Gardens

Soil

So, in case you're totally new to gardening, here's a quick head's up: soil types vary widely and can greatly affect your plants' success. If you're container gardening, make sure the soil you buy is for potting, and not for in-ground use. Potting soil drains better and one thing we definitely do not want is your sweet little garden bed to have poorly drained soil and rotted roots. You'll also likely see options for bagged mixes that are made for raised bed vegetable gardening, which is great if that's what you're doing. We start with an organic potting mix and add an organic fertilizer designed for whatever we're growing (whether it's vegetables, herbs, or ornamentals—there are fertilizers with ideal nutrient blends for each). A thorough mixing and a nice deep watering is all you need to get prepared for planting.

Watering

Depending on the size of your container garden, watering can be a fun little morning activity or a full-blown workout. Herbs typically need to be watered about once a week, but they'll slump a bit to let you know when they're thirsty and perk right back up with a proper watering. If planted in properly draining quality soil, fruit and vegetable gardens can suck up quite a bit of water; sometimes they need to be watered daily. Factors like sunlight and soil drainage can make this unique for each plant, so the best trick is to just stick a finger in it! Go about knuckle deep, and if you haven't hit a moist spot, it's time for watering. Ornamentals will vary in their watering needs, so make sure to familiarize yourself with the specifics of each plant you add to your garden.

Pruning

Pruning your garden regularly will encourage new growth! Mother Nature is extremely nice like that. When you prune, use sharp shears to trim newer growth at the center of the plants. Don't tear leaves off by hand, because clean cuts encourage better growth. Flowers will sometimes form on basil and other herbs, and while they are pretty, they are actually trying to sabotage you by taking the plant's energy. If you want to encourage new growth, it's best to cut or pinch off these flowers as they form. Guidelines for harvesting fruit and vegetables can vary widely based on the plant, and harvesting too soon or too late is an easy mistake to make, so be sure you look into the exact needs of whatever fruits and vegetables you grow.

CHAPTER 12

Three Easy and Afford-able Planter DIYs and the Houseplants We Love to Fill 'Em With

When we first started curating our plant collection, and it is quite a collection, we were pretty dumbfounded by how much the cute Instagram-worthy planters and pots can cost. Of course, basic terra-cotta pots are usually very cheap—but we wanted CUTER pots like blush-colored ones and fluted ones and ones that have little faces on them. There *are* pots that have little faces on them, by the way. But those other cuter options can be so costly. We made the tough financial decision early on that, while we would still allow ourselves to have a few of those special pots, the majority of our plant children would live in good ol' terra-cotta pots. We've got three DIYs to help you elevate the classic terra-cotta pot into something with a bit more style.

Planter DIY 1: Decorate Your Own Pots

A quick Google search for "blush planters" will give you no fewer than five billion results for cute-but-basic pink planters for forty dollars. Plus shipping! You can easily make these at home in any shade that your heart desires, for much cheaper and with very little effort. Paint is one of your budget bffs when it comes to refreshing basically anything, from walls to furniture to that smirk on your boyfriend's face—but right now? We're talking planters.

You'll need:

Terra-cotta pots with pre-drilled drainage hole

Exterior latex paint in the color of your choice

Foam paint brush

TIPS TO MAKE THIS AS CHEAP AS POSSIBLE

Use just a "sample size" of paint from a home improvement store here, which will cost you around five dollars.

Fill your pots with root cuttings from a recent propagation (we've got propagation instructions for you on page 133!).

1   Spread out a drop cloth or newspaper (assorted overdue bills or your ex's wedding invites also work fine here) in a well-ventilated area and lay out all of your materials.

2   Place your hand inside a pot and hold it up, then paint the entire exterior and bottom, rotating the pot slowly as you go to evenly coat the surface. Place the pot, top side down, on its lip and let it rest until dry to the touch, about 20 minutes. Repeat with the rest of your pots. Bonus tip: use painter's tape to tape off sections of your pots prior to painting to create different shapes or stripes.

3   Flip each pot so that it's resting on its bottom and paint the interior at least 1 inch (2.5 cm) down (the rest will eventually be covered by soil when you plant something in there). Let them dry completely before using.

And now you've got yourself your very own painted pots. What to do with them? We might have a few ideas (that's us telling you to keep flipping the page to see the other DIYs).

Planter DIY 2: Floating Garden

In all of the rentals we called home before buying a place, only one had a "real" backyard. And that particular backyard had "real" terrifying rodents and old needles everywhere. We would've put the time into cleaning it up, but we were honestly afraid to do it ourselves, and we were too shy to say, "Landlord, will you please hire someone to remove the needles scattered all over the backyard so we can plant a garden?"

Having zero or limited outdoor space doesn't mean you can't live your outdoor gardening fantasy—it just means you need to get creative with how you use what you've got. A vertical floating garden with mix-and-match planters is a fantastic way to make your small outdoor space shine, and it can be done for dang cheap. The one pictured here cost just twelve dollars. That's right, for the price of one very large burrito, you could have had an entire floating garden right outside your door.

You'll need:

Horizontal railing, wooden pallet, or hanging wooden craft board like the one pictured

Exterior paint and paint brush (if using a wooden pallet or board)

Rope or twine, if using wooden pallet

Nail, picture hanger, or wall anchor with screws, if using hanging craft board

Pot railing clips, widely available online (we used Terapotklip)

Standard terra-cotta pots with a lip on the outer rim (this is where the hook goes!), decorated to your liking—see previous DIY for painting and decorating (page 122).

1   Pick your spot! If you happen to have horizontal railings, then your decision's already been made for you. Otherwise, choose a part of your home or outdoor area that gets bright indirect light.

2   If using a wooden pallet or craft board, paint it and let dry fully before moving on. This can be a fun chance to add a pop of color, or to go for a classic vibe with a white paint. We matched our painted pots to the wall color and used a darker shade of a similar paint color for the wooden board to add contrast.

3   If you're using a wooden pallet for this DIY, such as the large 4 × 4-foot (1.2 × 1.2 m) ones used to transport retail products, you'll want to prop it up in your designated location and secure it with rope or twine to ensure it doesn't become top-heavy and fall forward when you add your planters. If using a hanging wooden craft board like the one pictured here, hang it with a nail or picture hanger secured into a **STUD**; or use a **DRYWALL ANCHOR** and screw if there's no stud in the exact spot you want to hang it.

4   Clip the railing clips onto your pots, fill the pots with soil and your plants, and arrange them as desired.

Planter DIY 3: Hanging Plant Window

Filling your windowsill with plants is lovely, but filling your window with hanging plants that flow gracefully downward and dance in the sunlight? Very, very lovely. We've always found hanging plants in our windows to create a relaxing mood, and in any window that doesn't require lots of privacy, they can even become your own living window treatment!

You'll need:

Low-profile mounting brackets for blinds and installation hardware (can be found in the window treatment section of most home improvement stores or online)

1-inch-thick (2.5 cm) wooden dowel cut to fit within the brackets (can be found at most craft stores or online)

Shower curtain rings

Hanging plant baskets

Planters—keep weight in mind! Opt for lightweight planters or, if using terracotta, stick to smaller pots that your dowel can support

Plants

1 If you have blinds installed in your window already, they most likely are in place with the use of window blind mounting brackets. If that's the case, you'll need to just unclip the brackets, slide out the blinds, and put them in storage, and then move on to step 2. If you don't have blinds, you'll need to install the mounting brackets in the top left and right corner of your windowsill.

2 Rest your wooden dowel in the mounting brackets and clip the brackets shut. Give the dowel a slight tug to make sure it's secure.

3 Attach the shower curtain rings to the top loop of your hanging basket and clip the curtain ring to the dowel.

4 Add your plants to your hanging baskets, and you're done!

NOTE: Our go-to hanging planters are simple macramé, because they're inexpensive and add a little bit of textural variance to a room. By no means are they the only option you have. We recommend scouting websites like Etsy and eBay, where there are many adorable handmade pieces. You'll be able to find hanging brass planters, rattan planters (totally on brand for boho rooms), and various natural wooden planters as well. You should get several hanging planters of varying lengths in order to create a flow of varying levels among the plants. You can always add length by tying string around the top hoop of a planter to extend it.

Our Favorite Houseplants

Plants. They're the quieter precursor to actual human, pooping, crying children! At least, that's how we treat them. Welcome to responsibility! The good news is, if they randomly die you won't be all *that* devastated and/or go to prison.

Mixed greenery around our home has been a must for us long before succulents and fiddle-leaf figs and Monsteras took over Instagram, and for good reason. Plants are affordable ways to add literal life and color to your home. They speak to responsibility and personality, and are constantly changing and growing, which adds an element of excitement. Waking up to new growth on your plant buddy? Feels great. And plants can be styled as decor in a million different ways. We're going to give you a rundown of our favorite green friends, and we'll even throw in a quick tip on making more plants from one big plant, via propagation! And p.s., don't you dare mention we told you this, but most of the big hardware stores let you return dead plants within ninety days, so hold on tight to those receipts, sweetie. If you see any plants you love in this chapter but can't find them at your local stores and nurseries, check out online nurseries that can ship to you (many of which are on Etsy or sell directly through their own online shops).

Pages 130–131 show a few of our favorite houseplants that bring joy into our hearts with their flourishing greenery and ability to make us forget all about the horrible, horrible outside world. We've included their common names (which may vary), their scientific names, and their water and light needs to help guide your plant care.

Plants that require **DIRECT LIGHT** will typically do best with 4 to 6 hours of unfiltered sunlight. These will thrive in unencumbered south-facing windowsills (in the Northern Hemisphere) that receive beams of sunlight. Plants that need **BRIGHT, INDIRECT LIGHT** will do splendidly several feet away from a south-facing window, but direct sunlight may scorch their leaves. **LOW-LIGHT-TOLERANT** plants can bring green life into even the darkest corners of your home, and if you live in a north-facing apartment with very few windows, or just have some corners of your home where very little light reaches, these are for you!

Plants pictured, from left to right: rattail cactus, baby rubber plant, rabbit foot fern, Monstera Deliciosa, fairy tale cactus

	NAME	BINOMIAL	LIGHT TOLERANCE	WATER
1	**Pothos, devil's ivy, ceylon creeper**	*Epipremnum aureum*	Indirect light, low-light tolerant	Keep soil slightly moist but not wet
2	**English ivy, common ivy**	*Hedera helix*	Bright indirect light, morning direct light	Keep soil slightly moist but not wet
3	**Bird-of-paradise**	*Strelitzia nicolai, Strelitzia reginae*	Direct light, bright indirect light	Drench and allow to dry
4	**Swiss cheese plant**	*Monstera deliciosa, Monstera adansonii*	Bright indirect light	Keep soil slightly moist but not wet
5	**Snake plant**	*Dracaena trifasciata*	Indirect light, low-light tolerant	Allow soil to dry completely between waterings
6	**ZZ plant**	*Zamioculcas zamiifolia*	Indirect light, low-light tolerant	Keep soil slightly moist but not wet
7	**Chinese money plant**	*Pilea peperomioides*	Bright indirect light	Keep soil slightly moist but not wet
8	**Figs—rubber tree, ficus audrey, fiddle-leaf**	*Ficus elastica, Ficus benghalensis, Ficus lyrata*	Direct light, bright indirect light	Keep soil slightly moist but not wet
9	**Spider plant**	*Chlorophytum comosum*	Indirect light, low-light tolerant	Allow soil to dry completely between waterings
10	**String of hearts**	*Ceropegia woodii*	Bright indirect light	Allow soil to dry completely between waterings
11	**String of pearls**	*Senecio rowleyanus*	Bright indirect light, morning direct light	Allow soil to dry completely between waterings
12	**Donkey's tail, burrow's tail**	*Sedum morganianum*	Bright indirect light, morning direct light	Drench and allow to dry fully between waterings
13	**Rattail cactus**	*Aporocactus flagelliformis*	Direct light	Allow soil to dry completely between waterings

Greenery as Decor

If you don't have a ton of wall art and decor you've collected over the years, finding the right pieces to complete a room can be intimidating. In our experience, art and most decor are best gathered over time. But if you want a finished space right now, plants come to the rescue. Whether you've got a big, empty expanse of wall, a shelf that feels a little bare, or a corner of a room that lacks excitement, the green friends have got your back.

Our favorite plants for styling on shelving or surfaces are trailing plants, like the *Monstera adansonii*, string of pearls, and, of course, our old friend pothos, whose big leaves and sheer dedication to not dying are truly inspiring. With their dangly bits and curious journey from root to leaf, they add movement and a touch of life to a space. If you're going to style a shelf or surface with multiple plants, stick to our tips on creating vignettes (page 70) and make sure you've got contrast in height, shape, and color.

Picking the Perfect Pot

When picking out a pot, consider how it will fit into your planned aesthetic, and also make sure there are drainage holes, which is something a lot of them lil' fancy pots you buy online will sometimes, inconveniently, not have. (Any excess water stuck inside your container can cause root rot, which is about as sad as it sounds.) Flip back to pages 122–127 for three DIY planters you can make yourself!

Propagation

If filling your home with plants is the ultimate way to create a gorgeous space on a budget, then propagation is like slapping on a discount code. **PROPAGATION** just means making one or several plants out of a single plant, and it's a very easy thing that feels very intimidating. The easiest and most common method of propagating houseplants is either by stem cutting or by dividing the roots of a plant. Stem cutting requires that you use a pair of sharp shears to cut a piece of a plant off to root on its own, while root division requires tugging the roots apart before planting the new individual plants in separate pots.

Typically, vining plants like pothos do well with stem cuttings, while root division is best for plants that have several different offshoots protruding from the soil, such as the ZZ plant. If you have a particular plant you're thinking of tearing in two, do a little research into which propagation method will work best for it.

DIY: Stem Cuttings and Water Propagation

Propagating plants in water from stem cuttings is our favorite method of propagation because you can see the root progress as it's happening and the whole plants-flowing-out-of-glass-vases thing is just beautiful to us. We love to keep a few plants actively propagating around the house to add another element of green—and for the excitement of playing clone scientists.

You'll need:

Plants for cuttings:
pothos, philodendrons,
and monsteras

**Extremely sharp shears
or a razor**

**Glass vase or jar with
fresh water**

Locate a node on the base of a vine or stem and cut just below it—nodes are a brown nub protruding from the plant and a likely place for new roots to develop. Place your cutting in fresh water near a window that gets bright indirect light and is free of major temperature fluctuations and drafts. Roots should begin to show within two to three weeks.

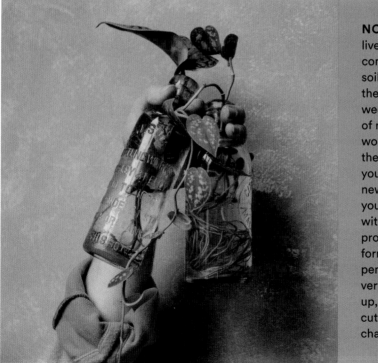

NOTE: Your new plant can live its entire life in just a container of water without soil, as long as you change the water about once a week, though water's lack of nutrients means they won't thrive as much as if they'd been potted in soil. If you do decide to plant your newly rooted plant in soil, you should transfer it to soil within about six weeks of propagation. Sometimes root formation just doesn't happen—that's okay; you're still very special to us—but heads up, you can do multiple cuttings at once to up your chances of success.

CHAPTER 13

Creating Personal Pieces for Your Home

The "Live-Laugh-Love" Deep State Decor Ring has had recent success ensnaring millions of Americans into love affairs with generic, mass-produced decor, and we're somewhat concerned. We don't want to shame you for filling your home with pieces you love, so if inspirational quote art is your thing, please ignore us, but we do have to ask—what does that globally marketable print have to do with you, and why display it in your home over objects *you* chose to save or capture during a moment in *your* life? And look, maybe it's not news to you that a sign reading "Live-Laugh-Love" has no place in a home that is intended to feel chic and personal, but we're talking about *all* generic art, including those hip and inexpensive framed prints sold at every department-store location from New York City to Bozeman, Montana.

That being said, we don't *always* love how personal pieces are incorporated into a home. There was a moment in the early 2000s when every suburban home's design went like this: beige walls, brownish granite countertops, and a black-and-white family beach photo in a hallway. So specific, yet so uninspired. Sure, it's often just photos of you and yours, but there's room to be creative with how you display keepsakes and highlight personal moments from your life story in a nongeneric, design-forward way.

For instance, hanging family photos alongside "real art" in a gallery wall or among more serious decorative items will serve the dual purpose of elevating your cherished memories to the level of art, and grounding any serious pieces by giving them a touch of your personality. One of our favorite images is a low-quality "hidden camera" image of us on a gondola in Budapest. We were in the middle of a massive argument about something tiny— one of those that happen after traveling with your partner for a few weeks—and when we got off the gondola we were met with a huge image of us, arguing, on the gift shop TV. It immediately ended our argument because we started cracking up. We bought a print of the photo for, like, four dollars, and it's one of our favorite travel photos we have together because it's so ridiculous. Framing it in an antique gold frame and adding it to a wall of art with similar styles of frames is our fun way of bringing character and memories to that part of our home.

We don't have kids yet, but when we do, we hope to frame and hang their doodles in gallery walls alongside more "serious" art. We think that's an incredibly fun way to tone down the stuffy capital-A Artiness by pushing the limits of what even counts as art and elevating our kids' hard work in the process.

Family photos, of course, aren't the only option for personalized decor. It's super easy to frame pretty much any flat object, like notes or letters, or even more obscure objects like a plane ticket from a special vacation, that movie stub from the first date you went on with your now-life-partner, or a piece of peeling wallpaper from your first home renovation. There are items all around us that have special moments attached to them, but they so often get shoved into nightstands and crap drawers because we don't know what to do with them. Our solution? Get to immortalizing their meaning via framing and incorporate these pieces in vignettes and clusters of art around your home.

Want some more obscure ways to bring personal memories into your home all while picking up a new hobby? Look no further . . .

THOUGHT STARTERS!

Cross-stitch: Once Grandma's hobby and now a fun way to add quirk and charm to sterile spaces. Cross-stitch Instagram is alive and well and can provide tons of inspo for creating your own personal pieces. One of our favorite accounts to follow? @badasscrossstitch.

Line drawings: Line drawings are drawings, usually portraits, made with a single line. It's become a popular piece of decor and can be a fun way to mix something trendy with something personal—maybe you try your hand at a line drawing of your cat or favorite human? Search for "line drawings" on Pinterest or Etsy to get the inspiration going. Use a blank canvas and black paint with a fine-tip paint brush to create a piece ready to be displayed on your wall.

Vacation or event framing: Collecting three, four, or more memory-evoking pieces from one event, like a birthday or road trip, and framing them all together can create instant interest and give you something to look at lovingly. Maybe you just got back from a road trip to Sedona and you have a hiking trail map, a postcard you never sent, and a receipt from a gas station with a funny name. Frame them all together to tell the story of your trip on a wall.

Grid of instant-print photos: Polaroid, Fujifilm, and other instant-print photo options have made a comeback recently and having the only copy of a photo feels so rare and special. Dedicate a whole roll of these photos to a particular time of your life or a specific event, and then you can easily buy a photo frame and mat of whatever size you want, arrange the photos on the mat, and hold each one in place with a single drop of glue. Then just place the glass and the mat back into the frame and hang it up.

DIY Scented Candles

Scent and smells are closely linked to your memories and emotions—there's some science about amygdalas and hippocampuses, but we both barely passed biology, so you're not gonna get the deep dive. The important thing for our purposes is that smell = memory. A spring vacation to, say, New Orleans, might have left you with the sweet smell of jasmine imprinted in the back of your mind, just waiting to be brought up again. Or maybe you remember the scent of lilies from your wedding day and would love to fill your bedroom with that same fragrance.

Well, luckily for all of us, making your own candles is actually wildly easy and can be very low-cost. While we are absolutely guilty of going on tipsy 10:00 P.M. online shopping sprees for incredibly expensive scented candles, we make many of our own candles, too!

The below DIY makes four 4-ounce (120 ml) candles but can be scaled up or down with ease.

You'll need:

Four 4-ounce (120 ml) candle jars or equivalent volume of old candle containers (see Notes for how to prepare them for use)

4 cotton wicks with wick stickers

4 wick stabilizers

A single burner hot plate (or an electric stove top)

A double boiler (you can find inexpensive double boiler attachments for a pot you already have)

16 ounces (455 g) soy wax chips or blocks

Instant-read kitchen thermometer

1 ounce (30 ml) candle fragrance oil (see Notes)

Wooden paint stirrers or chopsticks

1   Using your wick stickers, place the candle wicks in the center of your candle containers and put the wick stabilizers in place. If you don't have wick stabilizers or your stabilizer doesn't fit the shape of your candle jar, you can use popsicle sticks shaped like a hashtag to center the wick. For any container wider than 3 inches (7.5 cm) you're going to want more than a single wick.

2   Place your double boiler on your hot plate, put the wax chips in the double boiler, and turn the hot plate dial to high heat. Stick your temperature probe in to monitor the temperature.

3   Melt the wax to a temperature of 180°F (80°C) and remove from the burner, and use your thermometer to closely monitor the temperature. Let the wax cool to about 130°F (55°C), then add the fragrance. Adding a fragrance at too high of a temperature can cause your fragrance to burn off and be less potent, so don't be too eager here! Use a stirrer or chopsticks to stir for at least a minute, making sure the fragrance is evenly distributed throughout the wax.

4   Once you've stirred in the fragrance for at least a minute, pour it into your containers, being careful to not disturb the positioning of the wick.

5   Let the wax cool until solid before moving the candles and allow them to sit for 24 to 72 hours before burning—this is known as "curing" and will produce a more fragrant candle with a stronger **SCENT THROW** (how far a scent can travel within any given space).

CANDLE-MAKING SECRETS THAT WE LEARNED THE HARD WAY SO YOU DON'T HAVE TO

Safety First. We try to avoid out-of-control fires whenever possible, so we're using an electric burner and double boiler here, as they are essential for making this a fire-safe project.

Picking Candle Fragrance Oils. You can find plenty of sellers online offering different fragrances and fragrance blends. Many will be blends of synthetic fragrances, or blends of synthetic fragrance and essential oils. Our preferred fragrance supplier is the Flaming Candle (theflamingcandle.com), as they've got a pretty solid selection of quality fragrances. Avoid using essential oils alone, as they burn off super quickly and don't create a very pungent scent, but you can mix essential oils with synthetic blends to help round out other fragrances and provide a nice **COLD THROW**, the scent of an unlit room-temperature candle.

Fragrance Load. Different waxes can hold different fragrance loads, which is the amount of fragrance used in relation to the amount of wax used. Check the instructions from your wax supplier to see if they specify a certain fragrance load that you should be using, otherwise stick to our 1 ounce (45 ml) of fragrance per pound (455 g) of wax ratio.

Reusing Old Candle Containers. You can reuse any old burned-out candle containers you like, and we often do this! To get rid of the old wax, just fill them with boiling water, let them sit for a few minutes, and discard the water. Dry thoroughly before pouring your new candles.

Flower Drying and Pressing

It took us a truly very long time to appreciate flowers, many many years in fact! They always seemed so . . . froufrou? And expensive? Like, why do we need this costly pretty thing that will quickly turn into a once-pretty now-dead thing—gently reminding us of the passage of time whenever we lay our eyes on it. But the thing that changed that for us was realizing even dead flowers could be a thing of beauty.

If you've been given a floral arrangement from someone special or plucked some flowers out of a bouquet at a friend's wedding, flower drying or pressing is the perfect way to encapsulate those memories and turn them into gorgeous pieces of decor. Yes, of course, these DIYs are also absolutely great for any flowers you may buy for yourself or steal from your neighbor's yard.

Flower Drying

You'll need:

Flowers (use flowers that are on their way out but still have some life to them, avoid flowers that have already begun to shed petals or droop)

Pruning shears

Cotton twine

Remove any leaves and trim the stems to your desired length. Tie a string around the base of the bouquet and hang it from a curtain rod or rail where the flowers can be left undisturbed. Let dry for 3 to 4 weeks before putting the flowers in vases for display, hanging around the house, or framing.

NOTE: Not all flowers press well. In general, the best flowers are already flat and have just one or two layers of petals. Think along the lines of daisies, asters, and cosmos. Dense flowers like roses or peonies will not press well and are best dried.

Flower Pressing

You'll need:

Flowers with or without stem (see Note)

Parchment paper

Clothing iron

If your iron has a steam compartment with water, remove the water and dry thoroughly. Set your iron to medium heat. Working on a heat-safe work surface, place your flower(s) between two pieces of parchment paper. Gently press the iron down on the flower for 20 seconds, remove the iron and let the parchment cool completely. Repeat for four or five cycles, monitoring to make sure the flowers do not begin to brown. Different flowers will press better than others, and some may fade significantly during pressing—do a little experimentation before pressing any flowers that are of significant value to you! Let the flowers rest undisturbed for 72 hours before peeling off the parchment paper and framing them or using in other decorative projects.

CHAPTER 14

Yes, You Should Change That: Light Fixtures and Other Stuff You're Maybe Not Thinking About

We've been renters for most of our adult lives and have documented all of our home projects and redesigns on our blog. Other than an unsolicited "I hate it!" one of the most common comments we'd get whenever we'd make a big change is: "I wish I could do this, but I rent," and then we'd get to say, "Actually, we rent, too!" Until we bought our first home and started tearing all the walls down. Now we just have to be like, "Sorry!" But, really, the quickest and easiest refreshes (that can still deliver big change) are projects that many renters can tackle, and homeowners, too, can use these ideas to easily modify their spaces without diving into full reno mode.

While it's certainly true that renting can limit what you're able to do in a space during a redesign, sometimes a little sweet-talking your landlord is all you need to coax them into letting you work on your place. Painting was just our first venture into making a rental feel like home. From there it grew and took on a life of its own.

Whether you're a renter or a homeowner who doesn't want to deal with a major renovation right now, here are some of our tried-and-true methods to customizing a space without making major or permanent changes.

Light Fixtures

Not owning a property never stopped us from getting rid of the horrible light fixtures that landlords want their tenants to suffer under. A great light fixture can follow you from a rental to wherever you end up; in our case, we managed to hang a chandelier in three rental apartments before finally buying and moving into our first home—and we're still loving it. Switching out light fixtures is incredibly easy, likely something a landlord won't have an issue with or even notice (as long as you replace the original when your lease is up), and whether you own or rent it can completely change the look and feel of a room. We'll help walk you through some options and give you a step-by-step guide to replacing fixtures yourself.

The primary types of light fixtures are **CHANDELIERS**, **PENDANTS**, **SCONCES**, and **FLUSH MOUNTS**. Chandeliers and pendants hang from the ceiling by a chain, cord, or downrod. Chandeliers have multiple bulbs on one single fixture, and pendants house just one light bulb. Sconces are fixtures that get mounted to the wall, and while it's very lucky

We used the same light fixture in two rooms of ours that were stylistically very different. Investing in light fixtures you love can be a long-term renter's best friend. Pictured here is the Fontainebleau Chandelier from Sazerac Stitches.

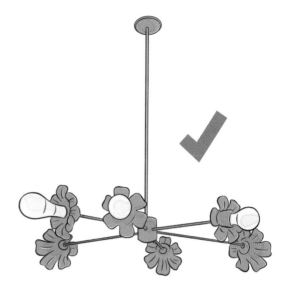

if you've got a **JUNCTION BOX** exactly where you want to hang a sconce, that's less likely than with ceiling fixtures. Some sconces are available with cords that plug into regular electrical outlets—no hardwiring required, you just need to secure them into place on the wall, maybe with a cute side table and decor to hide the cords. Finally, a flush mount is kind of like a sconce on the ceiling. It's a decorative fixture that doesn't drop down with a down-rod or chain, like pendants and chandeliers do. Flush mounts are appropriate for lower ceiling heights where you need the head clearance—consider replacing the boob light in a rental bedroom with a beautiful flush mount for a quick upgrade.

Light fixtures can lead the way in setting a room's tone. Lighting is one of the first details we decide on when designing a new space, and it often helps inform our other decisions. An elegant chandelier can immediately take a room into the realm of formal modern Victorian sitting room. Basket pendants to frame a couch can set you up for a chill boho den. Don't be afraid to make bold choices here—too often we see lighting decisions that were obviously made on a last-minute run to Home Depot, but unique pieces from platforms like Etsy, small independent makers like our trusted Sazerac Stitches, or authentic vintage finds can add major charm to a home.

How to Change a Light Fixture

Note: This is probably the only DIY in this book that could literally kill you, and we can't have that happening, so if this is something that you are uncomfortable with, pay the extra cash to have a handyman or electrician handle this—or just learn to love the lighting you currently have. Otherwise, follow the instructions extremely carefully.

Most important: Turn off both the circuit breaker and the light switch, not just one or the other.

Second most important: We're only talking about switching fixtures on an existing junction box here. Don't attempt to add a new junction box or do any other wiring modifications yourself, unless you know what you're doing and your local guidelines permit it.

You'll need:

A ladder tall enough to reach your fixture

An assistant

Voltage tester

Screwdriver (most commonly Philips #2 and potentially a flathead for the cover plate fastener)

Your replacement light fixture

1 **Shut it off:**

With the light fixture on to confirm the bulbs are in working order, turn the breaker off. Then double check you've switched the right breaker by flipping the interior wall switch on and off again. Have your assistant check behind you, because it's best to be sure when electricity is involved! Use your voltage tester to confirm there is no current running through the wires. Once you're sure there is no electricity going to the fixture, the wires are safe to handle.

2 **Remove the bad:**

Loosen the **COVER PLATE** and slide it down to reveal the **CROSS BAR** attached to the junction box. Behind the cross bar you'll find the wires, likely tucked away; pull these down so you can handle them.

You'll see three pairs of wires: One that is black or red, one that is white, and a third that is green or copper. Remove the rubber caps connecting the fixture's wires to the **HOUSE WIRES** of the junction box and unwind them from each other. Start with the black or red, and finish with the green or copper.

Your existing light fixture should have Phillips head screws holding its **CROSS BAR** in place. Unscrew those while your assistant supports the weight of the fixture.

Once the fixture has been unscrewed, your assistant can set the old fixture aside.

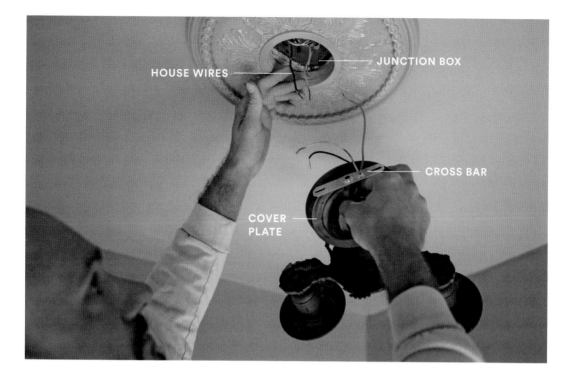

HOUSE WIRES

JUNCTION BOX

CROSS BAR

COVER PLATE

3 **Bring in the good:**

Have your assistant hold the new light fixture in place while you screw the cross bar to the junction box.

Starting with the green or copper pair, and finishing with the black or red pair, connect the wires from the fixture to the corresponding wires in the junction box. Twist the copper centers of each pair of wires around each other, and cap off each set with a rubber cap. Safety first: If your electrical box or new light fixture doesn't have wires that match up to each other or to the instructions we've given here, you should stop and get professional help to make sure your replacement is electrically sound. This can sometimes be an issue in older houses and buildings. It's less common but not impossible in newer homes.

Make sure the rubber caps are secure around each pair of wires, then tuck the wrapped pairs of wires back into the junction box. Slide the cover plate up and tighten the fastener to keep it in place.

And there you have it! A new beautiful light fixture ready to illuminate your now-perfect life.

STAY GROUNDED

This instructional assumes that the fixture and junction box both have three wires—the white "neutral" wire, the black "hot" wire, and the green or copper "grounding" wire. Sometimes the fixture itself will not have a grounding wire, but instead a green grounding screw on the cross bar (labeled in image above). In these cases the grounding wire from the junction box should be wrapped around the screw and the screw tightened securely so that the fixture is properly grounded.

DIY Decorative Picture Frame Molding

Picture frame molding, thin molding that is arranged into square or rectangular shapes like a picture frame, is just one of many ways you can style molding on a wall, but it's one we love for how it immediately adds charm to a room across many different design styles, and because it's relatively easy to do and budget-friendly. Cheap and easy—kind of our thing! This is a great DIY for homeowners wanting to give their home a relatively inexpensive upgrade, or any long-term renter with a relaxed lease who is committed to making their place pop off. We've got your full go-to guide for how to install this style of molding in your own home, and at the bottom of the DIY see our notes for how to alter this slightly to be more renter-friendly.

You'll need:

Painter's tape

Tape measure

Decorative molding to fit your planned designs (see step 2 for measuring tips)

Miter saw

Brad nailer and nails

Spirit level

Paintable caulk

Primer

Paint

Paintbrush

1   Use painter's tape to tape out the size and shape of the planned decorative molding around the entire room. If you know the exact decorative molding you want to use, use a painter's tape that is a similar width to help give you an idea of proportions (for instance, the molding we wanted to use was $\frac{5}{16}$ inch, so we used a $\frac{5}{16}$-inch-thick tape for this part).

2   Find the linear feet of your molding by adding together the length of each piece and use this to determine how much you'll need to order. Keep in mind when measuring: Joining two pieces at a 45-degree angle means you should account for the longest span of molding. If you're super new to making these kinds of cuts you're basically bound to mess some of them up, so order about a 15 percent excess to save yourself a trip to the store later.

3   Use your miter saw to cut your pieces to the desired length. If your miter saw is new to you or an item you're renting, you can find a video tutorial on YouTube that teaches exactly how to do angled cuts. We'd get into it here, but really a video tutorial is how you'll learn this the best.

Continues

NOTES: Follow all safety guidelines that come with any power tools you use and wear protective gear when necessary. Goggles and a dust mask are useful when making cuts, and you may also want noise-reduction ear plugs or earmuffs.

For renters wanting to do this project, we recommend skipping the caulking in order to make removal easier and less messy. When you need to remove the molding, you just pry it off and fill the tiny holes in the wall with spackle. Just a heads up, skipping the caulk may result in a slightly visible gap between the wall and molding, which aesthetically isn't ideal but might be fine by you, if it makes for an easier removal.

4 If you're planning to paint these suckers in a different color or finish than your walls, now's your chance to prime and paint! If you're painting these the same color and finish as the walls, move on to step 5 and prime and paint the molding once it's installed.

5 Level and tape measure in hand, begin your install. We used adjacent walls and windows to help give us exact distance measurements for where the pieces should go, but you could also use a yardstick and pencil to sketch on the wall as your guide. For any pieces longer than 36 inches (about 90 cm), this is easiest as a two-person job—one person to put the piece in place and hold it down, and one person to nail it in. Use your brad nailer to nail each piece of molding on both far ends to keep it in place, and then also nail every 12 inches (30 cm) along the molding. As you install, continually measure or use your sketched lines to make sure your wood isn't bowing. If it is bowing out, you'll need to firmly slide it back to where it needs to be when nailing.

6 Once all of your molding has been nailed, follow up by caulking the edges with paintable caulk. You should also use the caulk to fill any visible nail holes. Let the caulk dry fully before priming and painting!

Cabinet Hardware Knobs and Pulls

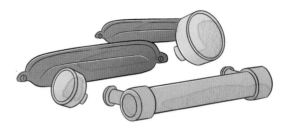

KNOBS, the cabinet handle with only one attachment, can be easily switched out with a Phillips head screwdriver. With **PULLS**, it's about 90 percent the same deal, but having two points of attachment means you need to get an exact measurement of the distance between the centers of the two screws when shopping for a replacement. Look for the **CENTER-TO-CENTER** measurement when shopping for your pulls and be aware that these measurements must be exact. There's not really an agreed set of standard measurements. If you own your home, it's easy to fill the old holes with wood filler, sand and paint the cabinet or drawer to match, and drill new holes for the pulls or knobs you like the most. For renters, you'll most likely want to match the existing holes, so just be aware you might be looking for a pull that's got a center-to-center measurement of 3¼ inches (8 cm) and find that a 3½-inch (9 cm) replacement won't work.

Unscrew the ugly bad bad stupid hardware that you hate and replace them with the new beautiful ones that you love, and it's as simple as that. If you're doing this as a renter, store your landlord's hardware in a Tupperware or other container and stuff them in the darkest part of your closet until it's time for you to replace them on your way out.

Your most stylistically versatile cabinet hardware options will be ones with a metallic finish. Chrome and brass are classic options, but matte-black metal hardware can give you a nice modern contrast to lighter-colored cabinetry. As for shape, the path of least resistance is to complement what your cabinets are already doing. If you've got sleek, sharp cabinets with clean lines, hardware with simple, modern shapes are the way to go. For something more traditional, maybe Shaker-style cabinets or cabinets with beveled edges, you'll want to choose something softer, rounded, or even ornate. Cabinet hardware is often an easy target for trends that get really old really quick, like the leather pull trend that came about with the modern farmhouse design era and just won't die. The good news is, since they're so easy to change out, you can feel free to follow hardware trends and whims as much as your time and budget will allow.

Window Treatments

If you're not into those plastic **BLINDS** we all love spying through, or if you're dealing with **DRAPES** that smell like Grandma in an upsetting kind of way, window treatments are fairly easy to remove and replace. All you need for that removal and install is a drill, and maybe a ladder, depending on the height of the window. An old stand-by is a simple pair of **CURTAINS** hung from a curtain rod—a good rule of thumb is for your rod to extend about 6 inches (15 cm) past the edge of your window on either side. In general, floor-length curtains are considered the gold standard, but for a window in a high-traffic area or in a house with pets that will, uh, pee on them, having your curtains fall just beneath the windowsill is completely fine. Consider adding a touch of drama and elegance with floor-length velvet curtains, or going airy and ethereal with sheer

lace ivory curtains that provide privacy without blocking out natural light.

ROMAN SHADES in a huge variety of styles can be custom-made by many online retailers to give a more minimal and sophisticated look, and even just quality wooden blinds are going to be a big step up from shoddy plastic window treatments. Select Blinds is an online retailer we often use, as they make quality custom pieces and have huge sales. Like all decor, window treatments can be your chance to further tie in color or pattern, like picking a non-dominant color in your rug as the color for your window treatments—this causes the eye to keep moving from the ground up and can help make a room feel complete—or a pattern such as plaid that can act as its own bold accent in a space. And the fabric is just the start! Hardware—the rod and **FINIALS**—can be anything from natural wood to matte black to an aged brass. Use these details as a chance to bring a room together; for instance, picking out light-stained wooden hardware to complement your rattan coffee table. If you've got a window that doesn't require privacy (for instance, if it opens up to a private backyard), consider forgoing window treatments altogether to let in as much natural light as possible. We did this in our current bedroom and love how the natural light fills the space and that we're woken up with the sun. This could also be your opportunity to fill your windowsill with hanging plants, which you can read more about on page 127.

Wallpaper

When done right, wallpaper can be a room's jaw-dropping design element that will make anyone who enters the space say things like "I am but a lowly peasant when it comes to home design; please teach me your ways." It can add color, pattern, and even texture to a space, serve as the perfect backdrop for your mid-workday selfies, and be that little extra something that brightens all the moments spent in any given room. While we love traditional wallpaper that adheres to walls with a **PASTE-THE-WALL** or **PASTE-THE-PAPER** method, it can be a bit tricky to do on your own. It also isn't easy to remove so we're gonna go ahead and file traditional wallpaper under "not renter friendly."

For renters or anyone looking to DIY wallpaper with relative ease and without spending many hundreds or thousands of dollars, we typically recommend **PEEL-AND-STICK WALLPAPER**. Peel-and-stick wallpaper has a pretty bad reputation that it may have deserved at one point, but these days there is some quality stuff out there that can bring a dramatic change to any space. If you're unfamiliar, peel-and-stick wallpaper is the type of wallpaper that can be easily removed without damaging the wall behind it, so it's practical for renters or anyone averse to commitment. Get creative with peel-and-stick wallpaper by using it to set off specific smaller areas of a wall, like the portion of the wall behind a workspace, floor-length mirror, or dresser. This is a cheaper option than covering an entire wall or entire room and can create just as big an impact by designating distinct zones. We recently used a tropical peel-and-stick wallpaper to upgrade our home bar by applying it behind the shelves—a $75 upgrade that changed the whole room.

If you have a smooth ceiling, this may be the perfect spot for your peel-and-stick wallpaper! Ceiling accents can be especially effective if you happen to have a high ceiling—say, 10 feet (3 m) or higher. A bold ceiling choice will instantly draw the eye upward and call attention to all that breathability.

A word of warning, though: Adhesives used in peel-and-stick wallpaper can be sensitive to heat and humidity, causing warping, so avoid using these products in places like bathrooms. A couple of our favorite traditional wallpaper makers are Graham & Brown and Divine Savages, and you can find quality peel-and-stick wallpaper from Tempaper, Carter + Main, and Spoonflower.

The hand-painted exterior mural is by artist Faye Bell. Check out all of her work at FayeBell.com.

CHAPTER 15

So, You Want to Renovate a Vintage Camper?

The year was 2017. We were living in the pink rental house and dreaming of a day when we'd own our very own home. We ran the numbers, smoothed our shirts, and tried to channel Humans Who Can Get Approved for a Mortgage for a meeting with a loan officer. When it came down to it, our income and credit weren't gonna cut it. Pro tip: If you're googling "what is a credit score" discreetly at the desk of a loan officer, it's maybe not quite time to buy. We were due for several more years of renting while we continued to grow our business, checking account, and credit scores. So, in true "us" fashion, we did none of that and instead bought a camper—a tiny home on wheels that we could actually afford. Purchased sight-unseen and shipped from West Virginia to New Orleans. A choice!

We'd spent months scouring online listings for vintage campers, places like eBay and Craigslist and Facebook Marketplace. There was a decrepit little cutie in Mississippi we could've gone to see, but the owner seemed threatening, and the photos were just grainy enough to be creepy, so we let it pass. There was another camper, an Airstream look-alike that upon closer inspection turned out to be a tiny toy collectible. And finally, we laid our eyes on a 1969 Globestar camper named Rosie.

8:39

She's going to need a lot of work, I'm just letting you know up front.

11:12

That's exactly what we're looking for!

- How to tile a wall?
- How to build a bed?
- How to make concrete countertops?
- What does mold smell like?
- Does lead paint have a smell?
- Camper smelly, what do?

And the list goes on. Removing the fabric seats got rid of the smell, by the way.

After about two months, Rosie was done. She wasn't going to win any best-in-show awards, but she was cute and useful and, most important, ours.

Wanna tackle your own camper reno? Keep reading; we got you!

Four thousand dollars and one week later, Rosie was on our doorstep, in her full glory, just staring at us. We were so ecstatic. WE OWNED A THING! It wasn't a big thing, it wasn't exactly in good shape, but it was *our* thing! And then we needed to learn how to renovate a vintage camper.

We were working on a tight budget, so we turned to skilled friends and DIY video tutorials to kick-start Rosie's makeover. Our carpenter friend Chad came in clutch with developing a plan for triangle wood floor-ing, and we also hired him to reconstruct the dining table with beautiful cypress. Our artist friend Faye kindly agreed to paint the exterior pattern, which was so gorgeous and absolutely worth five times what she charged us (thank you, Faye!!). Our favorite local lighting duo Sazerac Stitches was able to help build custom lights for the space. We paid our friends in both money and traded favors and skills (like photography!) to cover these items and a few other things that needed to be done. For the rest of it, we turned to internet research.

Before and after of Rosie's bed: The space originally had a bunk bed with a pull-out sofa bottom bunk and a fold-down top bunk. We removed the top bunk and installed a mattress as the main bed, which could get dressed up with plenty of cushions to act as a sofa or daybed during the day. Having spaces that are able to easily convert from one use to another throughout the day is key to living in any small space, whether it's a camper or a studio apartment.

Before and after of the kitchenette: We wanted to preserve and highlight the original vintage range oven and hood, so we went with creamy white colors for the cabinets and backsplash that would make the beautiful rich yellow colors stand out, and complemented them with brass hardware and lighting to tie it all together. Whenever we're designing a space that has interesting original elements—whether it be a vintage oven or a brick fireplace—our goal is to put them center stage, because they're what will make the space feel truly unique.

When Shopping for Your Camper

Set a Firm Budget (Actually)

We had $7,000 to spend on our camper project after months of saving, and we couldn't go over, like, at all. For the whole $7K we could've found something in decent shape but wouldn't have been able to afford to customize it or do any necessary repairs. On the other hand, we saw campers that were under $2,500 but they were more trouble than they were worth. So, we went with something in the middle, at $4,000, that would give us the remaining $3,000 to work with for fixes and custom touches.

Red Flags

The biggest things to avoid if you're working on a tight budget and don't want surprise costs are water damage, poor axle condition, and, of course, any obvious issues with propane lines, electrical wiring, or plumbing. Water damage can often require replacing entire portions of the roof or siding and potentially flooring, which will eat up your budget. Axle damage isn't that uncommon in older campers, but it can be an expensive fix and is also not a terribly exciting thing to spend money on. Finally, propane, electrical, and plumbing issues will all likely require that you hire out help. Not all fixes to those items are deal breakers, but it's

a good idea to have an inspection and quote done prior to purchasing if you suspect anything is wrong in any of those areas.

Location

After we searched in the New Orleans area, and eventually the entire Gulf Coast, we finally expanded to the entire country, which is when we discovered Rosie in West Virginia. Through websites like uShip, you can post large items—everything from furniture to campers—and have different shipping companies and individuals bid on shipping them for you. Having an item like this shipped (or in our case, towed) will be expensive, so keep that in mind when budgeting.

When Planning Your Remodel

Congrats! You've got a camper! Now what? We followed the same workflow as we do for any big remodel: develop a scope of work, edit the scope as needed to fit your budget, organize your tasks into a concrete schedule, tap into community resources (online or IRL), and get to work.

Build Out a Project Scope

Make a line item for every single thing you want to change—everything from big items like flooring to small items like cabinet hardware. Now you have the barebones of a project scope, and it's time to develop a design plan! Head to Part 1: Design (page 17) to establish your design direction. Armed with the project scope and design you can flesh out the specifics of where to allocate your remodel budget.

Join. Internet. Message Boards.

Join some of the vintage camper Facebook groups and subreddits to become a part of the camper community. We know, we know. Reddit and Facebook are terrifying places. But we promise that you can visit semi-anonymously without getting involved in the conspiracy threads by just focusing on what brought you there: vintage camper remodeling. Subreddits and Facebook groups are at times chilling for their bleak representation of the human mind, but this step is pivotal to getting info directly from people who've done exactly what you're doing. Just ignore the trolls.

Get to Work

With your scope, design plan, schedule, and resources, it's time to do the damn thing. It can be stressful, but don't forget to enjoy this process! We look back on our renovation with nostalgia for the time we spent learning how to do this new thing together, and we just try to block out all the times we would lay on the dirty floor at the end of the day and mutter, *"What the hell are we doing?"*

And now you have a camper! We took our inaugural trip to the foothills of the Smoky Mountains and had a lovely time. Wherever you go on your first trip, using your new camper will be a learning curve, so take notes while staying in it for any practical adjustments you might want to make before the next adventure.

Before and after of the dinette: We removed the upper cabinets to make the dinette feel more open—working with limited space often forces the choice between functional storage and that little extra smidge of breathing room. Since this would be more of a weekend getaway than a permanent home, we went with the latter. Oh, and see that little grated cabinet on the bottom right? That was a makeshift kennel for our dog, Fox, to curl up and nest in!

PART 3

Entertaining

Okay, we know "entertaining" and "hosting" are . . . stuffy terms? But, really, we're just talking about any time you welcome anyone into your home—whether it's a dinner party, your annual summer solstice backyard ritual, big events like a baby shower, or even just having a few friends pop in for takeout and wine. Regardless of what it looks like or how formal or casual it is, the most important thing about entertaining guests in your home is making sure that everyone feels comfortable and taken care of, so that nothing inhibits the joy of being together and sharing whatever it is you're sharing. We hope you agree that this is the moment the rest of this book has been leading us to.

CHAPTER 16

Our Entertaining Philosophy

When you've got people over, you're in charge of setting the mood for the gathering. You've put all this time into making your place feel especially yours, and now you get to share your home with your friends and family. So throughout this section, we're going to walk you through the steps of making your space as inviting as can be—from setting the table to prepping delicious snacks, drinks, and recipes.

Like good design, we believe good entertaining calls for character, charm, and comfort to be the stars of the show. No one wants a sterile gathering, and taking the few small steps to get the mood just right can make for a memorable and enjoyable time spent with your people. Depending on who you're having over—maybe it's that bff you used to get drunk with in college, or maybe it's your new boyfriend's parents . . . *ahh!*—edit our tips to your needs. Also, we're not following formal "etiquette" here; that stuff is hoity-toity BS, so please feel free to put your elbows on the table, talk about politics if you want, and set the knives and the forks wherever your little heart desires.

Dark and Stormy— Batch Style (page 218)

Do

Be a good DJ. Create or pick out a great playlist that fits the mood of the night. Speakers synced up throughout the home is a great way to set the mood early on, and Bluetooth speakers are an easy and affordable way to do that. But even if all you have is a laptop, make sure some music is playing. See page 173 for some of our favorite Spotify playlist recommendations.

Let 'em know what you're making. This can be an opportunity for guests to flag any dietary restrictions they have but can also help guide them if they're bringing along a side. Speaking of, have some ideas ready if they ask what to bring!

Set an easy menu. If you're making more than three multi-step dishes (and you're not a professional chef), you're probably overcomplicating things, and no one wants a flustered host—they want to spend quality time with you! Don't be afraid of challenging yourself, if that's something you enjoy, but keep it manageable.

Have bevs on deck. Plan beverages that pair well. Whether it's cocktails (page 211), wine (page 187), or just a simple lemonade, don't forget that drinks are part of the meal.

Keep the hunger at bay. Give your people something to shove in their mouths as soon as they walk in. See page 179 for our hot tips on making a thicc snack board. It'll appease anyone who shows up hangry, buy you time if you're running behind, and maybe even be a conversation starter, like, "Are Brazil nuts really from Brazil, or like, what's really going on here?"

Keep everyone out of your way. For any event where your guests will be milling about and talking to one another (like a birthday party or reception), try your best to have a drinks station outside of the main kitchen area. This will keep everyone out of your damn way, giving you access to use the kitchen for anything that might come up—like your baker friend insisting her famous apple pie be heated in the oven before anyone eats it.

Don't

Don't forget the sexy lighting (except in utility areas like the kitchen). Lamps, wall sconces, and even strip lighting placed behind credenzas and media consoles are all better options than overhead lighting for creating a cozy atmosphere. If you have a chandelier over your dining table, use low wattage bulbs, a dimmer switch, or smart bulbs that you can dim for an appetizingly warm glow.

Don't diss takeout. Don't be afraid to supplement any of your cooking (or, hell, all of it) with prepared food or takeout. You're making pad thai but don't want to figure out how to do the spring roll appetizer? Get that part delivered and take some stress off yourself.

Don't let the music take control. For dinner parties and other intimate sit-down situations, popular current music or super-recognizable classics can be distracting to conversation. Some of our favorite relaxing genres are instrumental jazz/hip-hop blended playlists and soft tunes in languages we don't understand, like French sixties pop or bossa nova. Or just play more obscure songs—it's not about being hip, it's about making sure the music doesn't take over the moment. Now if you're having a dance party, this can easily be the exact opposite advice—don't let the hits quit. We haven't been to a dance party in maybe five years so please invite us.

Don't make it smell weird. Don't burn scented candles near any food being prepared or served. Scents mix and mingle in strange ways, and we really want to highlight the scent of whatever's on the menu.

Don't be a neat freak. After dinner is over, if you can stand it, try to ignore the chores for a bit and relax into the moment with your guests. Picking up too early may accidentally crush the mood. (On the other hand, if you're ready for everyone to leave, just start cleaning up very loudly.)

CHAPTER 17

Cute Tablescapes for Cute Gatherings

Tablescape! It maybe sounds like something reserved for fancy occasions, but with just a little extra effort you can put together an arrangement that makes even the most casual gatherings feel a bit more special.

This doesn't have to be an expensive project. In fact, if you already own a few cute decorative pieces and are feeling resourceful, you can put together a stunning tablescape for little additional cost. Tablescaping, after all, is just a twist on curated vignettes, which you'll remember from our little convo about them (pages 70–71), and we'll be following much of the same approach.

Our whole thing, in case we haven't made it abundantly clear, is taking pretty casual approaches to the finer things in life. In that way we hope to make everyday moments just a notch more special, without the chance of making any given moment feel too stuffy or self-important. Whether you're creating an entire elaborate custom decorative spread for your dinner, or just lighting a couple of candles, it ups the experience to consider the presentation of the table. So go all out, or keep it minimal, but don't forget to put a little thought into your table!

Basic Elements of a Tablescape

- Dinnerware
- Flatware
- Napkins
- Glassware
- Centerpieces and arrangements
- Chargers and placemats (optional)

Pretty much every tablescape how-to on the internet will tell you that step one is picking a theme; then use glassware, dinnerware, napkins, and decorations that fit that theme. Sure, that's helpful, but the reality is that unless you're about to spend your cash on getting new dinnerware and napkins every time you want to have a dinner party—and have storage for, like, seven different sets of plates and napkins—it's not all that realistic. Let's go over the basics that you should have, standbys for your plates and napkins and glasses, and then we're gonna show you how we style the same setting up and down for different seasons, to give you some inspo.

Dinnerware

We're not saying to break out Grandma's fine china every time people come over, that sounds weird. But having a nicer "next step up" set of dinnerware adds a lovely touch to your get-togethers. We keep two sets of plates—one basic set from a big-box store for when it's just us two pigs schlopping up leftovers, and one for when we're being proper hosts who yes, of course, have the cool speckled ceramic plates from that small business you follow on Instagram. Whether it's something hip or something more classic, keeping an extra set of somewhat elevated dinnerware reserved for when you've got people over is always clutch.

Flatware

Like dinnerware, we like to keep a set of flatware just for entertaining—a vintage set of silver flatware that cost us forty dollars at a consignment store. We love how it brings old-school cozy charm to the table, but it's up to you whether you'd like to have the style of your dinnerware and flatware match instead of contrast each other! For us, even on the table, we find mixing new and old brings an eclectic and exciting blend that feels uniquely us and sends the perfect message of: "I put thought into this, but not too much, just relax and enjoy."

Dinner Napkins

Having decent cloth dinner napkins is a big plus! Making sure they don't have "fresh out the package" creases, or spots and stains is a bigger plus. Give your napkins a steaming or toss them in the dryer with a damp towel to help bring them back to life—and definitely wash them before their first use.

Glassware (Stemmed Glassware, Mix and Match?)

Are we doing mix-matched vintage? Are we doing more formal glassware and having a toast? Regardless of your table setting, which glasses you choose helps signal what the mood is. Our personal favorite is obviously mixing and matching vintage glasses, and we're sure that's no surprise to you at this point. If you've found some really cool glasses at an estate sale or vintage shop, they'll immediately add character and tell a story, while not reading as fussy.

Going for something more uniform? Sets of wineglasses can be found both new and secondhand for pretty great prices, but if you've never bought a set, it can be overwhelming. See page 197 for our tips on picking out wineglasses.

Arrangements and Centerpieces

Don't overthink this one! There are many deranged lifestyle bloggers (like us!) who forage their neighborhoods for flowers and branches and turn them into bountiful centerpieces. You don't need to know how to make a gorgeous bouquet to have a nice arrangement in the center of your table, even though that's always a nice touch—just a few fresh flowers in bud vases scattered about can do the trick! Our biggest tip? Seasonal flowers and foliage + a generic vase or ceramic bowl you can use all year round + a few decorative elements that fit the occasion = perfect centerpiece. We especially love tinkering with baby's breath, eucalyptus, and fresh-cut flowers like ranunculus for a relaxed bouquet. The more informal a gathering, the less glitzy a centerpiece should be.

Accessories

Once you've got all of the above figured out, you can focus on the finishing touches. Tapered candles in brass or ceramic holders make things extra cozy and intimate. Cardstock with handwritten names or jotted down menus make each place setting feel personal and bring a homemade vibe to an event. Eucalyptus at each place setting is a natural and gorgeous touch, and napkin rings can help further establish the tone of the evening. We love to include quirky items of decor that fit the color story of the tablescape and keep it from feeling too serious, like a vintage set of salt and pepper shakers.

Chargers and Placemats

These under-the-dinnerware mats tend to imply a more formal event. Personally, we prefer to skip them because when we have dinner the table is packed with family-style pots of food and it just doesn't feel like a good use of space to include them. That being said, if your table is delicate and vulnerable to getting beat up by kids, dinnerware, etc., chargers and placemats can act as protection. For us, they often (but not always) feel stuffy and dated.

PARTY PLAYLIST RECOMMENDATIONS

These are some of our favorite playlists, all available on Spotify.

- **Pollen,** by Spotify
- **Late Night Vibes,** by Spotify
- **Bossa Nova & Brazilian Jazz,** by masakic_records
- **The Motherfucking Future: The Nocturne Edit,** by Charli XCX
- **Dreampop/Shoegaze/Lo-Fi Buffet,** by Chris Chan
- **Smooth Crew,** by PREP
- **Outside Classics,** by Larry Little
- **Bedroom Pop,** by Spotify
- **French Flow—Lyricistes,** by Pixel Playlists
- **Chill Out & Electro—Summer Chill Mix II,** by Pixel Playlists
- **Instrumental Hip Hop/Chill Hip Hop/ Jazzy,** by alexcpc

Tablescapes for Every Season

So, with all that talk on tablescapes, here are a few seasonal ones we created to help inspire you! We used the same dinnerware, flatware, napkins, candlesticks, and glasses for each season to help illustrate how you can dress up a single set throughout the year, for informal or more formal gatherings.

Spring

Spring is a time for a clean, fresh approach to entertaining that incorporates lighter and brighter florals and table settings. Vases full of lush flowers and greenery and bud vases with interesting florals make a springtime brunch sparkle. Pop some Champagne, make our blueberry scones (page 245!), and require everyone to wear handmade flower crowns.

Summer

Summer = fun, and everyone knows it. Bring in brightly colored decor that utilizes natural elements like the leaves of a bird-of-paradise or banana tree to create a carefree tablescape that is perfect for even the hottest of hot summer evenings. Maybe consider getting a little campy like we did with the inclusion of a vintage fan and salt and pepper shakers shaped like sunbathers. Summer *camp*. Get it? Yellows, oranges, and pinks drive home the tropical touch we're leaning into here.

Fall

The line between a fall tablescape that says "I just love this time of year" and one that says "I inject pumpkin spice into my veins" can be thin. A mix of real gourds of varying size and shape scattered about does wonders, as do amber vases or glassware; mixing in natural white and ivory colors helps provide balance. And a good tip on keeping it tasteful? Avoid anything with an "autumn" or pumpkin print—we don't need prints or themes when we have the ability to create a real autumn moment using organic materials and proper item selection.

Winter

Nondenominational holiday eleganza is on the menu, and we hope you're ready for it. Whether you're a diehard evangelical (in which case, good for you for making it through this book, honestly) or you firmly believe absolutely nothing happens when we all die (bummer), the winter holidays allow you to take your decor over the top without feeling too gaudy—so go as big as your imagination takes you. For all you outside-the-box types, consider trying a fun twist like our desert winter–themed tablescape full of traditional holiday colors in an unexpected way.

Checklist for When Your In-Laws or Boss or Other People You Want to Impress Come Over

- [ ] **Wipe down your appliances** to free them of those stupid fingerprints—we guarantee you have stopped noticing them, but they're there.

- [ ] **Make sure all bathrooms have hand soap, hand towels, and toilet paper.** If guests use your personal bathroom, find a safe hiding place for your, uhhh, anything private, prescription drugs, and other weird topics you don't want them to broach.

- [ ] If your guests are coming over for a meal or to stay a few nights, **ask for a reminder of any dietary restrictions or allergies** to make sure everyone who arrives alive stays alive. We firmly believe the best guests are ones with a pulse.

- [ ] If your guests are staying the night, **wash the sheets in their room day of (you can always tell when sheets are freshly washed) and make the bed fresh before they arrive**. Because that's just nice. Also make sure to have enough (clean) bath and hand towels stocked in whatever bathroom they'll be using!

- [ ] If you want to go the extra mile, **add fresh-cut flowers in rooms you'll be entertaining in**. Your thriving house plants (that you learned how to care for on page 131) will impress, but something cut fresh in a vase feels extra thoughtful.

- [ ] If you were planning on starting an herb garden anyway (see page 112 for how to make one!), the day before guests show up is a fabulous time to **purchase your transplants and get to potting**. There's pretty much no chance you'll kill the seedlings before everyone assumes you're a perfect domestic genius.

Look at you, being a cute, good host and whatnot. You go!

CHAPTER 18

How to Make a Thicc Snack Board

Fun fact: We could survive on snack boards alone. For a low-key date night in, snack boards are unfussy and don't require actual cooking, and there's minimal cleanup. A snack board is easy to throw together, so it's a perfect indoor picnic for two with a bottle of wine.

Beyond date-night potential, having a baller snackboard at a party or casual gathering will make your guests be like: "Mmmm tasty, yummy little buffet of snacks!" We'll make one for casual things like an Oscars or *Drag Race* watch party, or a backyard birthday get-together. Or, if we're having folks over for dinner, we'll have one of these ready to snack on while we finish up the meal. Basically, all snacks all the time.

The only real rule we're setting is that your snack board should hit as many different flavors and textures as it possibly can. Crunchy things, chewy things, salty things, sweet things, acidic things, and fatty things.

This brings in balance and excitement and, while we don't generally recommend casting a wide net to people-please (everyone can sense that and will think you're fake) snack boards are an exception: Load them up with all the options to make sure everyone has something they like. For example, something sweet and crunchy, like candied pecans, something acidic and chewy, like sundried tomatoes, and something salty and creamy, like hummus. All of those items, along with our snackboard staples (meats, cheeses, and bready things—further expanded in the next few pages), come together to create a beautifully thicc snack board.

Meats

We usually aim for three meats of varying spice level and density. Some meats are spicier and harder than others—make your jokes but keep that in mind. For the mildest, go for a **SPECK** or **SERRANO HAM**. Both have a soft, melt-in-your-mouth texture. Next, something like a **SALAMI GENTILE** will have a touch of spice and a nice mid-range chewiness. Finally, a **SPANISH CHORIZO** or **CALABRESE SALAMI** will be tough and chewy and bring some heat to the table. If you really want to go the extra mile and spend a tiny bit more money, give spreadable meats some love (e.g., **PÂTÉ**, **TERRINE**, **MOUSSE**, or **RILLETTES**).

Cheeses

As with your meats, include as many or as few cheeses as you want, but we find a well-rounded starting point is to use three: something soft or creamy, something crumbly or crystally, and a mild-leaning blue cheese. For your soft cheese, **BRIE** is a crowd favorite. You could also go for another creamy and mild cheese like **DÉLICE DE BOURGOGNE** or **SAINT-ANDRÉ**. For your crumbly cheese, try an **ENGLISH CHEDDAR** or aged **GOUDA**. For blue cheese, we recommend milder options like **GORGONZOLA** or **BLEU D'AUVERGNE**. We are *huge* fans of blue cheese and always include it on a snack board, but funkier options like **ROQUEFORT** can be polarizing, so proceed with caution. There are so many options for cheese even at the most basic grocery stores, and it can get overwhelming real quick, so on pages 182–183 we've provided more fleshed-out info about what to look for at the cheese counter.

CROWDSOURCE THE BOARD!

Don't be afraid to be specific when friends ask you what they can bring! The easiest place for them to contribute is going to be on the snack board, because these ingredients don't require cooking or much prep at all. They'll feel confident they're bringing something that's wanted and essential.

Breads and Other Carbs

For the most part, bread and toast and crackers are the vehicle you use to transport the sweet gift of cheese (and other things) gently to your lips. Unless nobody is around, in which case we're all guilty of occasionally just shoving a chunk of cheddar into our mouths. Like with your meats and cheeses, try offering a few options for your breads. We always aim to have one tribute from three different arenas: fluffy, crispy, and hearty. Your fluffy options will be things like **FOCACCIA**, **CHALLAH**, and **BRIOCHE**. For crispy, we're pretty much talking crackers here. Classic **BUTTER CRACKERS**, **SALTINES**, or Italian **TARALLI** fit the bill. For the third option, we like to go for **BUTTERED TOAST POINTS** or something like a semi-soft **FRUIT AND NUT LOAF** with a chewy interior and tough crust.

Accoutrements

Accoutrements, a fancy word for "other stuff," is just everything else you find on a snack board that isn't cheese or meat or bread. You can 100 percent get creative here, but the main categories are going to be pickles, fresh fruit, nuts, and spreads. As far as fresh fruit, anything bite-sized and a little tart works well, such as berries, grapes, and cherries. Sliced Fuji apples and pears are delicious with a little honey and blue cheese on top. Add an unexpected element! Some of our favorite snacks that don't fit into any of those categories but are totally delicious to use on a snack board: potato chips, dolmas, crispy chickpeas, kale chips, raisins, and granola clusters. Listen to your heart.

To finish off your board, make sure there's also a proper selection of spreadable things. Our favorites to use are honey, jam, Dijon mustard, and butter. You can also look into combinations of those: honey mustard or honey butter, or a fruit mostarda (kind of like the love child of jam and mustard—our fave is peach mostarda, recipe on page 185). After you've got your spreads all set, your snack board is finally done. Your only mission now is to try out a million different combos of all your ingredients in search of the perfect bite. And save some for us; we're coming over!

No-Frills Guide to Cheese

Cheese is kind of scary! Much like wine, it can be intimidating to get familiar with the varieties of cheese and what makes them different from each other, or what flavors and textures to expect if you're buying before you're trying. Use the info here as your guide next time you're stuck face-to-face with a hundred cheese options and need to just pick a few!

Bloomy Rind Cheeses

These cheeses are ripened from the outside in, so as you get toward the center they tend to be softer, and possibly even runny. They're easily spreadable, generally mild in flavor, and we suggest placing them on a small dish to avoid a gooey mess.

- **BRIE**
- **CAMAMBERT**
- **SAINT-ANDRÉ**
- **DÉLICE DE BOURGOGNE**

Semi-Soft Cheeses

This category is defined more by texture than flavor; "semi-soft" means these cheeses have a soft but not spreadable consistency. These can vary greatly in flavor, so you may want to include more than just one on your board.

- **MUENSTER**
- **JARLSBERG**
- **HAVARTI**

Semi-Hard Cheeses

The largest and most popular category, semi-hard cheeses are the ones you're probably most familiar with. These are aged, but not for as long as hard cheeses; they can vary in flavor from mild to sharp and are always dependable crowd-pleasers.

- **CHEDDAR**
- **GOUDA**
- **GRUYÈRE**
- **EDAM**

Hard Cheeses

These are aged a pretty long time and have lost nearly all of their moisture. Often grated and used as a topping for salads and other dishes, these can be a delicious salty and nutty addition to your snack board.

- **MANCHEGO**
- **PARMIGIANO-REGGIANO**
- **PECORINO ROMANO**
- **GRANA PADANO**

Washed-Rind Cheeses

Funk alert! These are infamous for their funky tastes and smells. Some in this category have hints of B.O. and gym shoes. These cheeses are soaked, or "washed," in a salty brine (hence "washed-rind") that promotes the growth of some pretty stinky bacteria and mold. They can be really enjoyable, but you've been warned!

- **TALEGGIO**, arguably the mildest and therefore a good entry point
- **MORBIER**
- **ÉPOISSES DE BOURGOGNE**
- **LIMBURGER**

Blue Cheeses

Blue cheeses get their colored marbling from the type of bacteria used to mature them. These are easy to identify, but here are some popular ones (roughly organized from mild to funky):

- **GORGONZOLA**
- **BLEU D'AUVERGNE**
- **DANISH BLEU**
- **STILTON**
- **ROQUEFORT**

TIPS TO MAKE THIS AS CHEAP AS POSSIBLE

Start in your fridge! Given the endless number of options you have for things to include on your snack board, starting with what you've already got (maybe a block of Parmesan, a jar of pickles, some grainy mustard you can put in a cute dish) is a good way to cut down on unnecessary purchases.

Utilize your grocery deli. Instead of buying prepackaged meats that may offer a larger quantity than you need, start at your grocery's deli counter and ask if they can slice up the exact amount of meat you need for your board. Less waste, and money saved.

Bargain bin. Check to see if your grocery's cheese section has an "under $5 bucket" or similar scrap bin that's got loose ends and bits, sometimes called orphans—aww, wouldn't you just love to adopt them? They're perfectly fine cheeses that are left over from the cheesemonger's bigger cuts, and they can be the perfect amount to use on your board if you're serving more than one cheese.

Make what you can at home. Turn a baguette into crostini with just a little olive oil and some time in the oven. Make a cherry spread by sautéing cherries, sugar, and vinegar instead of buying a fancy jam.

PHYSICALLY ORGANIZING YOUR SNACK BOARD

Start from the center of your board and work your way out, making sure to weave each item around the next, creating a flow of deliciousness. Board shape and size are up to you, but we typically pick one that is *just* big enough to hold all the goodies—empty space on a snack board is upsetting. We typically start with a butcher-block board as our base and use pedestals, stands, glassware, ramekins, and bowls to create levels and separate items, which will also keep the eye moving around the various items and create excitement. Any particularly messy cheeses or things like butter should go on a smooth surface that can be easily cleaned, like marble or ceramic, and shouldn't be in direct contact with any

other messy things. If you splurged on a particularly nice cut of meat or other delicacy, highlight its glory with its own smaller dish on the board. As a general rule of thumb, anything that needs to be cut with a sharp knife, like a salami or a hard cheese, should be cut beforehand, and anything that can be easily cut with a butter knife or spoon should be left whole, with said knife or spoon placed beside it (although feel free to make a few starter cuts to get it going). A mix of precut and whole items can help add visual interest to your board and inspire guests to dig in—a board full of whole, uncut items may discourage guests from messing any of it up.

Easy Peach Mostarda

This peach mostarda is a sweet and tangy addition to a summertime snack board. The perfect bite? A piece of crusty bread, a smear of a soft mild cheese like brie, and a dollop of mostarda. Beyond snackboard potential, this mostarda works great on sandwiches or as the base for a salad dressing!

Takes 30 minutes
Makes 3 cups (710 ml)

2 pounds (910 g) peaches (about 8 peaches), peeled, pitted, and roughly chopped.

2 cups (402 g) sugar

1 tablespoon mustard seeds

1 tablespoon coriander seeds

1 teaspoon garlic powder

1 teaspoon mustard powder

1 teaspoon salt

⅔ cup (158 ml) white wine vinegar

⅓ cup (79 ml) white wine

Combine the peaches, sugar, mustard seeds, coriander seeds, garlic powder, mustard powder, and salt in a saucepan over medium-high heat, and cook for 10 minutes until the peaches begin to produce liquid and break down—you can assist this by gently smashing with the back of a wooden spoon. Add the white wine vinegar and white wine and cook for an additional 20 minutes, stirring occasionally, until the mixture begins to gel. Transport to your serving dish and let cool before serving. This can be made in advance and kept refrigerated in an airtight container for up to 2 weeks.

CHAPTER 19

No BS Guide to Wine

Years of rubbing shoulders with sommeliers, a stint working at a local wine shop, a general interest in all things
wine, a few hands-on visits to vineyards and wineries,
and an irresponsible wine budget have given us the ability to fool all of our friends and family into thinking we're
wine experts. And we do know a lot! But mostly we just
know how to find a fantastic, people-pleasing bottle of
wine for any time of day or occasion, for somewhere
between ten and thirty dollars, and we want to help you
do the same. There are entire libraries full of info about
wine and very many experts more qualified than we
are who give thorough details about the entire process,
history, science, and art of wine, but that's not
really going to help you buy the right bottle
for *tonight*, is it? We're going to give you
the quick rundown and help you walk any
wine aisle with the confidence to pick
something perfect.

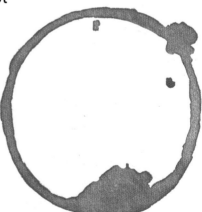

Anderson Valley doesn't just make incredible wine; it's also gorgeous. This was the view from our cabin on our first trip here together.

Shopping for the Right Bottle

You're face-to-face with dozens of bottles of wine at the store, trying to pick which one to grab. Should you go with the old standby or is it time to try something new? Is your wine-loving friend gonna judge you for what you pick? There are signs marking sections by varietal: Chardonnay, Cabernet Sauvignon, Sauvignon Blanc. But there are also signs marking sections by origin, too: France, New Zealand, Italy. This was going to be simple, but now it feels impossible, and are these wine labels mocking you?

To make things more complicated, price isn't necessarily a good indicator of a wine's quality—you can get a great bottle of wine for thirteen dollars, and a bottle of junk for twenty dollars. Our most time efficient recommendation for anyone afraid of overspending on crappy wine is to find a small, local, independently owned wine shop and do your wine shopping there. That's at least until you begin to grow your knowledge and get a better sense of what you like and how to find it in a sea of mixed-quality options. Small wine shops tend to be better curated than big liquor stores, and the staff tends to be more in the know and eager to help. If you live somewhere that doesn't happen to have a small, well-curated wine shop, no sweat, we can help guide you. To further simplify your shopping experience, any time you see a wine name **STYLED LIKE THIS** in this chapter, that is what will appear prominently on the wine's label.

SKIP THE STORE

If you find a bottle you love or visit a vineyard while traveling and really enjoy their product, consider joining the vineyard's wine club or buying directly from them online. Direct-to-consumer sales are always more beneficial for small vineyards and can sometimes save you money! We visited Bonny Doon Vineyard in Santa Cruz on a road trip years ago and fell in love with their quirky wines; we'll occasionally order a case directly from them. Some other favorite vineyards we've visited or ordered from are Navarro Vineyards, Martha Stoumen Wines, Ruth Lewandowski Wines, Rails Nap, and Ridge Vineyards.

BUT, GUYS, WHAT'S THE DEAL WITH "NATURAL WINE"?

Okay, wow, talking about natural wines is going to open a whole other can of worms that will quickly make this uncomplicated wine chapter *very* complicated. But, just so you know, **NATURAL WINE** is a loosely defined term that typically refers to wines made without much intervention from the maker. Synthetic pesticides, preservatives, and flavor additives are usually excluded or kept to a minimum, and the end result is basically just juice that's been allowed to naturally ferment. There's no one style to natural wines. They can be very refined like a conventional wine or have an earthy, funky, or sour character, with some natural wines even appearing slightly cloudy.

It's not a *new* way of making wine, but it is currently very trendy and also hotly debated among some wine circles, with many people praising it and others thinking it's subpar, rudimentary, or over-hyped. We love it, but it's likely not going to be a very common or easy to find on the shelves of your big corporate liquor store or grocery store. That's not to say they aren't available—plenty of winemakers are making what could be considered "natural wine" but aren't calling it by that lingo, let alone putting the term on the bottle. Knowledgeable salespeople at independent, curated wine stores should be able to point you in the right direction.

Ruth Lewandowski Wines makes incredible natural wines, so we order it online by the case.

Navigating the Wine Store

Here's the deal on how most wine stores, sections, or aisles are organized:

IN GENERAL, New World wines (the Americas, Australia, New Zealand, South Africa, China) are labeled according to the varietal (e.g., **SAUVIGNON BLANC**, **SANGIOVESE**, **TEMPRANILLO**) and Old World wines (basically just Europe) are labeled according to where they're from (e.g., **SANCERRE**, **CHIANTI**, **RIBERA DEL DUERO**). **VINICULTURE** laws across Europe control which varietals and wine-making styles can be used for wines bearing the names of different regions and **APPELATIONS**—and so the place name can actually tell you what kind of wine to expect, if you spend the time getting familiar with those laws and naming customs.

So, if you wanted a French Chardonnay and there is a sign for France and a sign for Chardonnay, you'd actually look under the France sign. Find a bottle of white that says "**BOURGOGNE**," "**MACON-VILLAGES**," "**POUILLY-FUISSÉ**" (these are just a few popular examples of French places that make wines with chardonnay)—they may not say "chardonnay" anywhere on the bottle, but that's what's in there, and you can expect them to be crisp and mineral driven. If the oaky chardonnays of California are more to your taste, check out the section labeled just "Chardonnay." You'll find mostly chardonnays from California, likely several options from Washington and Oregon, and potentially other New World regions.

Learning about all of the viniculture laws and the traditions of different growing regions

can certainly be helpful, but we promised a no-BS wine guide, so we're not going to categorize these wines by varietal, style, or region of origin; instead we'll dwell on the super-scientific measurement of ⁓vibe⁓. Scan our vibe list on the next few pages and use our short descriptions to pick whichever one fits the event or occasion you're headed to or the mood you're in. Oh, and we're not trying to bankrupt you! All of our suggestions can be found for less than thirty dollars a bottle if you do some searching.

READING IS FUNDAMENTAL

Pay a *lot* more attention to the words on a label than to the design. Typically, the more specific the location listed on the front label of a bottle of wine, the higher quality you can expect. This expectation has a lot to do with the concept of **TERROIR**. For example, usually French **RED TABLE WINE** is of lesser quality than **BURGUNDY/BOURGOGNE**, which would be made entirely of grapes from the Burgundy region. **GEVREY-CHAMBERTIN** would be even higher quality, containing all grapes from that single village in Burgundy, and **CHAMBERTIN CLOS-DE-BÈZE** would be even higher quality than that, containing only fruit from a specific grand cru vineyard in the village of Gevrey-Chambertin, making it a top-tier wine for that region. Obnoxiously, wine regions all over the world have completely different ways of structuring their hierarchies, which is part of what makes wine so hard to learn.

Wines for Balmy Summer Afternoons

Crisp and refreshing wines for those hot AF summer days when water just doesn't cut it. These white and rosé wines are cool and crisp with a little acidity but not too too much. Poolside or oceanside is the obvious setting of choice, but these are also good for picnics, sunset walks, sitting sensibly on white couches, and being the main character in a miniseries about rich white women and murder.

Alsace Wines

GEWÜRZTRAMINER, **PINOT GRIS**, **MUSCAT**, **PINOT BLANC**, and **RIESLING**. Each of these white varietals has a distinct personality, from floral and thick to lean and sharp, but they all feel like a refreshing cool breeze when you could totally use it. Wines from Alsace will list the varietal on the label (unlike most Old World wines), and you can count on them to start at around twenty dollars per bottle. Most Alsatian white wines are bone dry, though some can have a sweetness that gets nicely balanced out by their high acidity, and still others are so sweet they could be served as dessert wines.

White Burgundy/Bourgogne

These 100 percent Chardonnay bottles are much less in-your-face than the New World chardonnays at the same price point. They can have bright notes of apple and pear and will typically not have as pronounced of an "oak" flavor as in American chardonnays, if any at all. **POUILLY-FUISSÉ**, **MÂCON-VILLAGES**, (and a slurry of other wines that start with a **"MÂCON"** prefix like **MÂCON-LA ROCHE-VINEUSE**), and **ST-VÉRAN** are fantastic and can be found in most wine shops at affordable prices. **CHABLIS** gets a special shoutout for the region's unique soil and aging in stainless steel, which gives it a super crisp minerality that sets it apart from other white wines from Burgundy.

Txakoli/Txakolina (cha-co-lee-na)

Crisp and slightly bubbly, these taste like a fancy Mediterranean yacht party in a bottle, speaking as people who have never been to a fancy Mediterranean yacht party. These wines come from Spain's Basque country and are less frequently stocked in your average store, but when you find a bottle, you've gotta take some home. Look for white and rosé options.

Wines for Unwinding

Light- to medium-bodied wines for enjoying with snacks after work or while soaking in the tub. These are for those afternoons where you just need to open up a bottle to take the edge off, *or* for something to pair with snacks or appetizers when you've got people over. Also great to pair with lighter meats, seafood, or veggie entrees like mushrooms and eggplant, fresh herb sauces, and even some cream-based sauces.

Albariño

A satisfyingly refreshing white wine that sits pretty far on the acidic end of the scale, making it a balanced pairing for salty snacks or, famously, for seafood dishes like ceviche and really any shellfish, including shrimp, oysters, and octopus or squid. In Spain Albariño will typically have "**ALBARIÑO**" on the bottle, and in Portugal (where the grape is called alvarinho), it's made into some of the very best **VINHO VERDE**.

Beaujolais

This region makes red wines from 100 percent gamay noir grapes that can be bright and simple or serious and complex, but always light bodied and fruit driven. Bottles that just say **BEAUJOLAIS** can be incredibly affordable and of decent quality, but some higher-tier wines from this region can also come reasonably priced: Look for **FLEURIE**, **CÔTE DE BROUILLY**, **BEAUJOLAIS-VILLAGES**, and **MORGON**.

Rosés from Southern France

CÔTES DU-RHÔNE, **CÔTES DE PROVENCE**, and **LANGUEDOC**. You can expect these rosés to be well balanced, dry, and best served slightly chilled. Rosé is made all over the world, but some of the best is made in Southern France, in the regions of Provence and Languedoc-Roussillon and the southern part of the Rhône region. Some higher-prestige wines in our price range are made in the subregions **BANDOL** and **TAVEL**.

WATCH OUT

Don't confuse standard **BEAUJOLAIS** with **BEAUJOLAIS-NOUVEAU**. There's nothing *wrong* with **NOUVEAU**, but it's more of a sweet party-chugging wine, closer to grape juice in taste. **BEAUJOLAIS-NOUVEAU** is released on the third Thursday of November, in the same year the grapes were harvested, and when it runs out, it's out till the next year.

Wines for Staying In with Your Dog

Your go-to unfussy, everyday, and anytime wines. These are your everyday wines, best enjoyed walking around the house in your caftan or while sitting on the couch watching reality TV. Just pour a glass, and maybe even throw in an ice cube while you're at it. Kidding . . . but not really. Do what makes you happy, and if that's putting ice in wine, go right ahead.

California Chardonnay

The loaded minefield of the wine world, California **CHARDONNAY** can be some of the worst wine available if you're not careful. Lots of the affordable chardonnays made in California are bottles of straight up oak juice, which isn't, like, good. At all. But when you find a good chardonnay, full bodied and full of flavors like vanilla and pear and honey, you will be like: "wow wow wow." The best advice here is to shop in your small local wine shops like we mentioned above, where you can find one or two California chardonnays that work for you and stick with them if you don't want any surprises. One of our favorite producers of this style is LIOCO Wine Company, so if you see it on your shelves, give it a try!

Sauvignon Blanc

In addition to lime/pear/peach fruit notes, sauvignon blanc can have an underlying grassiness that makes it polarizing—you'll likely either love it or hate it! With medium-high acidity, it's a great go-to pairing for your Thai or Vietnamese takeout or any other spicy or herby meals. If domestic sauvignon blanc is something you often drink, consider branching out to the Loire Valley in France and Marlborough in New Zealand for some of the world's most popular sauvignon blanc that can still be found within our price range. **SANCERRE**, **POUILLY-FUMÉ**, and **TOURAINE** are some French options. You can also check out white **BORDEAUX** (sometimes written **BORDEAUX BLANC**), which is made by blending sauvignon blanc and another two varietals, sémillon and muscadelle.

Pinot Noir from Oregon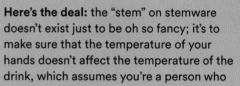

With a distinct earthiness, these wines tend to be closer in flavor to French **BURGUNDY/ BOURGOGNE** than to **PINOT NOIR** from California, which by comparison is brighter and fruitier. Still expect a medium-light body, and a more affordable price tag than the French stuff. For anyone looking for an easy-drinking red, Oregon pinot noir is your new best friend. Want to try some of our personal faves? Check out wines from the **WILLAMETTE VALLEY**.

AW HELL, I NEED TO BUY SOME WINEGLASSES, BUT I DON'T KNOW WHICH ONES TO GET!!

Shopping for a set of wineglasses can feel like taking a personality test, and wow, that's a lot of pressure. Stemmed, unstemmed, cabernet sauvignon glasses, Burgundy glasses, chardonnay glasses?

Here's the deal: the "stem" on stemware doesn't exist just to be oh so fancy; it's to make sure that the temperature of your hands doesn't affect the temperature of the drink, which assumes you're a person who actually cares about that (you can read more about wine temperatures on page 199). If you aren't so particular and enjoy your wine at any temperature that is liquid, then unstemmed is a totally fine option, if that's the look you prefer.

As for the shape of the glasses: You'll see glasses labeled as "red" or "white" or for specific styles of wine like "Bordeaux" or "Burgundy." There's science behind it and if you want to nerd out about it, check out the further reading section on page 249. For our part, we just recommend picking one style that is a medium-width, not super wide and not too narrow. Typically, a general "cabernet" glass or "standard red" glass will work great for all your wine-ing needs.

Candlelit-Dinner Wines

For those nights you put on that red lipstick and order the steak. These medium-to-full-bodied red wines are bold and, there's no other word for it, kind of sexy? While it's perfectly fine to drink them alone, they pair well with a hearty meal—whether it's a rib-eye from your favorite steak spot or just a couple of slices of greasy pepperoni pizza with friends.

Côtes-du-Rhône

These red blends are medium-to-full-bodied bombs of red fruit flavor with a hint of baking spice. Made with the varietals grenache, syrah, and mourvèdre (sometimes called GSM blends or Rhône blends), basic **CÔTES-DU-RHÔNE** can be reliably decent and start around twelve dollars, and the (generally) higher-quality **CÔTES-DU-RHÔNE-VILLAGES** can be found under twenty dollars. Occasionally you can score village-level **GIGONDAS**, **VACQUEYRAS**, and *rarely but not never* the big daddy of the Southern Rhône, **CHÂTEAUNEUF-DU-PAPE** (unfortunately pronounced: "Shat enough doo pop") for less than thirty dollars.

Bordeaux

Full-bodied and well-balanced with subtle fruit notes like dark cherry but noticeable minerality as well, these are red blends of mostly merlot and cabernet sauvignon with smaller or less common inclusions of cabernet franc, petit verdot, carménère, and malbec. Just a step above the basic **BORDEAUX** and **BORDEAUX-SUPÉRIEUR** (starting around fifteen dollars per bottle), you can find affordable **GRAVES**, **SAINT-ÉMILION**, and **SAINT-ESTÈPHE**.

Rioja, Ribera del Duero 🍷

RIOJA are medium-to-full-bodied red wines made with 100 percent tempranillo that are oaky and fruity on the basic end (**RIOJA CRIANZA**) and getting more complex with selective aging (**RIOJA RESERVA**) until they become intense, musky, earthy things (**RIOJA GRAN RESERVA**). **RIBERA DEL DUERO** is also made from tempranillo (though the varietal is called tinto fino in that region) but will have a more concentrated and intense flavor profile than rioja.

Chianti, Chianti Classico, Sangiovese 🍷

These are super-flavorful and savory medium-bodied red wines, and if you want something to go with your Italian restaurant staples (think lasagna, pizza, chicken Parmesan), there are simply no wines that do it better than these girls. Italian Sangiovese wines will have a regional name—**CHIANTI** and **CHIANTI CLASSICO,** starting at around twelve dollars (and there is not necessarily a quality difference between them). Take a slight step up and you've got **ROSSO DI MONTAL-CINO, ROSSO DI MONTEPULCIANO,** and **VINO NOBILE DI MONTEPULCIANO.** Sangiovese is rarely grown outside of Italy, but there are a few from California that will have **SANGIOVESE** on the label.

Whenever we travel to a winemaking region, we love spending an afternoon touring vineyards and visiting tasting rooms. While touring Ste. Chapelle Winery in Idaho (yes Idaho has wine!), we got to watch and taste wine at different steps of the winemaking process. Here, merlot grapes are being sorted by hand to remove any bad-looking berries.

Cozy Sweater Wines

The snuggliest of snuggly wines, for everyone who loves sweater weather.
These are the strong, warm hugs of the wine world that you'll want if you're ever having wine by a fireplace as the snow flurries begin to get heavier outside, or something stupidly romantic like that. They can fill you with a tingly feeling like when someone scratches your head.

Syrah/Shiraz and the Northern Rhône

Generally big, bold, dark red wines, syrah and shiraz are two names for the same grape, but if you see **SYRAH** on the bottle, it's safe to expect a serious earthy wine, while **SHIRAZ** (preferred term in Australia but appears on some South African and U.S. wine labels, too) typically implies a more new-world, fruit-forward style. French Syrah from the Northern Rhone region like **SAINT-JOSEPH** and **CROZES-HERMITAGE** can occasionally be found under thirty dollars but more reliably we can find affordable syrah from Washington, where it will still have that dark, earthy, and wild thing going on, as opposed to the fruitier persona of Californian and Australian syrah/shiraz.

Cabernet Sauvignon from California

The OG "Big Red" for most Americans, it's the epitome of bold, intense, fruit-forward flavor that's often compared to **BORDEAUX**— the two have a rebellious-younger-brother/ snooty-older-brother sort of relation-ship. **CABERNET SAUVIGNON** and other **BORDEAUX-STYLE BLENDS** from California can be hella yummy, but there are plenty low-quality bottles at the same price points as high-quality ones, so go with a recommen-dation from a local and independent wine and liquor shop or trusted wine snob! Some of our favorite American cabernet sauvignon producers are Billhook and Alexander Valley Vineyards.

Zinfandel/Primitivo

This chewy, complex, and exciting red wine is lush and fruity, often with notes of baking spice and pepper. It's another two names/one vari-etal situation—**PRIMITIVO** is used in Italy and **ZINFANDEL** in California. If you like Zinfandel and Primitivo and want to branch into more obscure territory, try the related Croatian vari-etal **PLAVAC MALI**, occasionally shortened to **PLAVAC**. (The *c* makes a *ts* sound in Croatian, so it's pronounced *plah-vahts mah-lee*.)

Popping Bottles

Sparkling wines for toasting your best friend's job promotion, or an easy way to make a regular Tuesday a little fun. Everyone knows the queen bee of bubbles, **CHAMPAGNE**, and that "it's not really Champagne unless it's from Champagne." Well, rarely do you find true Champagne for less than thirty dollars, so we cost-conscious drinkers usually get our fix elsewhere.

The easiest trick to buying quality non-Champagne sparkling wines is to stick with wines made in the same method as Champagne—the **TRADITIONAL METHOD**. Sometimes "traditional method" will be printed on the label near the wine's name, although likely it would be in the language of wherever it's bottled.

The traditional method is known as *méthode traditionelle* in French, *método tradicional* in Spanish, *metodo classico* in Italian, and *klassische Flaschengärung* in German.

Two of our favorite traditional-method wines are crémant and cava, both of which are typically much cheaper than Champagne.

HOT TIP FOR BUBBLY WINE

Pair it with salty fried food. French fries and fried chicken are seriously some of the best food pairings sparkling wine could ever ask for.

Crémant

Crémants will always have a region name tacked on the back. **CRÉMANT D'ALSACE**, **CRÉMANT DE BOURGOGNE**, **CRÉMANT DE LOIRE**, and **CRÉMANT DE LIMOUX** are the most common. Look for both white and rosé options!

Cava

This style is popular for a reason. **CAVA** is generally *much* more affordable than champagne, and while it tends not to have the same complexity, it can still satisfy that itch for some quality sparkling wine.

The TRADITIONAL METHOD is only one of many ways winemakers add bubbles to their wines. Here are some sparkling wines of two totally different styles.

Pét-Nat or Petillant Naturel (literally "naturally sparkling")

These wines finish their fermentation in the bottle, causing a natural sparkle from the trapped CO_2. It's considered one of the earliest methods of making sparkling wine, and will typically have softer bubbles, with a wide variety of flavor profiles. You'll sometimes see this style referred to as the ancestral method, or *méthode ancestrale*, on wine labels.

Tank Method/Charmat Method Sparkling Wines

This is how **PROSECCO** is made, along with sparkling red **LAMBRUSCO**, German **SEKT**, and many sparkling wines from the U.S. These wines have lower-pressure carbonation, which for us drinkers just means looser, softer bubbles. They tend to have a slightly higher sugar content as well—you might even want to call them "sweet and loose" when they're out of earshot.

WINE TEMPERATURE

If you're having your whites right out of the fridge or your reds right off the shelf, they may not be at their ideal temperature, and temperature affects flavor. Every specific style of wine has a precise temperature where it's at its absolute best, but here's a very general guide:

TYPE	IDEAL TEMPERATURE	HOW TO GET THAT, APPROXIMATELY
Red	60–65°F (15–18°C)	• Refrigerate for 45 minutes from room temperature, or • Place in freezer for 30 minutes, or • Toss in fridge 1 to 2 days before enjoying and remove about 20 minutes before serving.
White, rosé	48–55°F (9–13°C)	• Refrigerate for 2 hours from room temperature, or • Place in freezer for 45 minutes, or • Store in your fridge 1 to 2 days before enjoying and remove about 10 minutes before serving.
Sparkling	40–48°F (4–9°C)	• Refrigerate for 3 hours from room temperature, or • Place in freezer for 1 hour, or • Store in your fridge at least 1 full day and serve immediately.

For short-term storage, say a month or so, wine is fine stored in a standard kitchen refrigerator. Longer than that and the cork may start to dry out, which is no good! That'll ruin the wine before you even get to open it. If you're collecting and aging special bottles, the best place to keep them is in a wine cooler. If you don't have one or don't want to get that serious, keep bottles in a cool, dark place, and on their sides so the cork has contact with the wine inside.

Spring Sangria (page 206)

CHAPTER 20

Getting a Crowd Tipsy on a Budget with Sangria

Sangria is one of our go-tos for large-batch drink preparation, and it has so much more potential than the syrupy red stuff you drank in college. We've got a template for you to use when crafting your own sangria, as well as a few seasonal recipes to try out. Each recipe can be easily doubled, tripled, or quadrupled, depending on how much fun y'all are trying to have. And keep in mind, while there's no reason to spend big bucks on a bottle of wine you'll be adding lots of stuff to, you should still pick out something halfway decent, 'cause a bad sangria hangover is truly very upsetting.

YOUR SANGRIA TEMPLATE

1 (750-ml) bottle wine

½ cup (120 ml) hard liquor or 1 cup (240 ml) liqueur (or some combination of both)

¼ to ½ cup (60 to 120 ml) liquid sweetener (simple syrup, agave nectar, fruit juice, or sweet liqueur)

Sliced fruit

Herbs or spices, optional

About 12 oz (355 ml) or 1 can chilled carbonated beverage

You're going to mix all that together in your serving pitcher with ice and pour into your eager guests' glasses. When using fresh fruit, herbs, and spices, you can let your sangria sit in the fridge for 2 to 24 hours (before adding any carbonated ingredients) to let the flavors meld, but feel free to serve immediately, too—it'll still taste great.

A Sangria for Every Season

Taking our above template and plugging in some personal favorites, we've got four sangrias for you—one for each season!

Spring Sangria

This bright and refreshing white sangria has plenty of floral and citrus notes to wake you up from your little winter bear nap.

Serves 6 to 8

1 (750-ml) bottle crisp white wine, such as **VINHO VERDE** or **ALBARIÑO**

½ cup (120 ml) gin (a floral gin like **HAYMAN'S OLD TOM GIN** works well here)

½ cup (120 ml) elderflower liqueur, such as **ST. GERMAIN**

½ cup (120 ml) honey syrup (1:1 blend of honey and water, boiled until honey dissolves)

2 lemons, sliced into cross sections

2 limes, sliced into cross sections

12 ounces (360 ml) sparkling water, chilled

Fresh mint or basil, for garnish

Combine all the ingredients besides the garnish in your serving pitcher, give it a stir, and serve over ice. Garnish with mint or basil.

Summer Sangria

If you're not drinking this while sunbathing on a gorgeous seaside chaise lounge in Ibiza, you're not doing summer right. It doesn't matter if the Ibiza part is just in our imaginations!

Serves 6 to 8

1 (750-ml) bottle **CÔTES-DE-PROVENCE** rosé, or other dry rosé

½ cup (120 ml) **CAMPARI**

¼ cup (60 ml) light agave nectar

2 ruby red grapefruits, sliced into cross sections

2 limes, sliced into cross sections

12 ounces (360 ml) grapefruit soda beer, such as **STIEGEL RADLER**, or a nonalcoholic grapefruit soda of your choice, chilled

Fresh rosemary, for garnish

Combine all the ingredients besides the garnish in your serving pitcher, give it a stir, and serve over ice. Garnish with rosemary.

Summer Sangria

Fall Sangria

We don't really get a true fall where we live so we love to compensate for that with this spiced, brandy-spiked sangria—it's refreshing but still offers all the flavorful vibes for a full-blown Christian Girl Autumn.

Serves 6 to 8

2 pears, thinly sliced

2 apples, thinly sliced

¼ cup (60 ml) lemon juice

½ cup (120 ml) brandy

½ cup (120 ml) cinnamon simple syrup (see recipe)

2 (16.9 ounce/½ liter) cans dry cider

1 (12-ounce/360 ml) can ginger beer, chilled

Cinnamon sticks, for garnish

Add the fruit and lemon juice to your pitcher and gently mash with a wooden spoon. Add the brandy, cinnamon syrup, cider, and ginger beer and stir well. Fill with ice and serve each glass with a cinnamon stick garnish.

Cinnamon Syrup

Makes 2 cups (475 ml)

2 cinnamon sticks

2 cups (400 g) sugar

In a saucepan over medium-high heat, bring 1 cup (240 ml) water and the cinnamon sticks to a boil. Add the sugar, whisk to dissolve, and remove from heat. Let steep for 1 hour before discarding the cinnamon sticks and using the syrup. Store in the refrigerator in an airtight container for up to 1 month.

Winter "Sangria," aka Mulled Wine

Mulled wine is canonically winter's sangria. It's basically a traditional red sangria plus spices like cinnamon and star anise, all warmed up and served in a mug.

Serves 6 to 8

2 oranges, peeled and chopped (reserve peel)

8 to 10 whole cloves

1 (750-ml) bottle French or Spanish **RED TABLE WINE**

½ cup (120 ml) dark rum, such as **MYERS'S RUM**

½ cup (110 g) packed dark brown sugar

4 cinnamon sticks

3 whole star anise

⅛ teaspoon ground nutmeg

1-inch (2.5 cm) nub fresh ginger, sliced in half

Stud the orange peel with your cloves by piercing the skin of the orange with individual cloves—this helps keep the tiny spices from floating away and winding up in the finished product; plus it looks cool. Combine all the ingredients in a pot over medium heat, bring just to a simmer, and stir to ensure the sugar is fully dissolved. Serve warm in mugs. We like to serve individual mugs with chunks of ginger, spices, and studded orange peels all together, for a rustic touch. Feel free to strain out the solids before drinking if you prefer!

CHAPTER 21

Building a Home Bar: How to Get Your Friends to Stop Nagging You to "Go Out"

We both spent years in the New Orleans service industry, so we have plenty of experience making and enjoying cocktails, saying "no, thank you" to mid-shift party drugs, and building our own at-home arsenal of liquors, aperitifs, and bitters to tinker with based on what we were learning at work. While these days we're more likely to reach for a bottle of wine when drinking at home, we still like to break out cocktails when we have friends over. Mixing drinks can be a fun, interactive part of entertaining done with relative ease if you've got the right tools on hand. Let's check out some of the cornerstones of building your at-home bar, including tools and ingredients every home bartender should have. The brands we're recommending in this chapter are what we think are the best quality for reasonable prices, mostly falling between twenty and forty dollars a bottle.

Checklist for Basic Tools

☐ **Shaker:** There are several shaker options, but the kind we recommend is a set of two steel shaker cups, occasionally referred to as a **STAINLESS STEEL BOSTON SHAKER** or a **SET OF SHAKING TINS**. It's easy to use, easy to clean, and has a large enough capacity to hold two to three drinks at a time.

☐ **Strainer:** We recommend a **HAWTHORNE** strainer, as it's great for either stirred or shaken cocktails (unlike a **JULEP** strainer, which won't strain out the citrus pulp or ice shards in any of your shaken drinks). Bonus points for also grabbing a **FINE-MESH** strainer, which is useful for prepping batches of citrus juice or straining out herbs or spices from homemade flavored simple syrups.

☐ **Double jigger:** This two-sided measuring tool helps you get your proportions right when making cocktails. The standard size has notches measuring ½ ounce, ¾ ounce, 1 ounce, and 1½ ounces (15 ml, 22 ml, 30 ml, and 45 ml). There's also a version with notches measuring ¾ ounce, 1 ounce, 1½ ounces, and 2 ounces (22 ml, 30 ml, 45 ml, and 60 ml), which is a less common find, but we prefer it because many classic cocktails call for 2 ounces (60 ml) of **BASE LIQUOR**.

☐ **Barspoon:** Mostly for stirring cocktails, but this is sometimes also used as a measurement tool equal to a teaspoon, "a barspoon of syrup," for example.

☐ **Mixing glass:** While we're not super into cocktail-mixing showmanship, a nice crystal mixing glass is a beautiful investment that will elevate the look of your bar area and serve as your dedicated glass for stirred cocktails.

☐ **Citrus peeler:** Much easier to use than a paring knife, a citrus peeler comes in handy for creating elegant and simple garnishes for your cocktails.

KEEP IT CUTE

But let's be real: The actual most important bar tool for your purposes is a bar cart, or some other disgustingly cute way of organizing and displaying all your spirits and glasses and other tools. You can have the most impressive bar tools in the world, but if you can't post a cute pic of the setup to Instagram, does it even matter? Will anyone even want one of your cocktails? No, likely not. See our tips for styling your bar cart on page 75!

Checklist for Essential Non-Liquor Ingredients

- [ ] **Simple syrup:** This mixture of sugar and water commonly used in cocktail making is available to purchase, or incredibly easy to make at home (see how on page 227).

- [ ] **Citrus:** Lemons are crucial—lemon peel is used for garnishes, and lemon juice is used in plenty of cocktails. Lime juice is also common in cocktail recipes, and orange peel is another common flavor-enhancing garnish.

- [ ] **Bitters:** Basically, the seasoning of the cocktail world, they have highly concentrated flavors meant to be used in tiny amounts, typically just a few drops. The most common are **ORANGE BITTERS** and **ANGOSTURA BITTERS**, but there are endless flavors, from peach to cherry to chocolate to habanero.

- [ ] **LUXARDO cherries:** These are the fancy dark syrupy cherries and *not* the neon red guys. You can use Luxardo cherries and/or their syrup in a variety of cocktails, like Manhattans, Aviations, or your own original creations.

- [ ] **Fizzy things:** Club soda, ginger beer, tonic, and sparkling wine are common additions to cocktails or can be used as "mixers" for anyone needing their vodka soda, whiskey ginger, gin and tonic, or the like.

YOU'RE ALSO GONNA WANT:

Fortified wines and liqueurs are great to have on hand for lots of classic cocktails, from a Martinez to a margarita. Below are a few of the essential categories and our favorite brands for you to use as your starting point! Note that fortified wines, like vermouths, should be refrigerated after opening.

- Sweet vermouth: **COCCHI VERMOUTH DI TORINO, CARPANO ANTICA,** or **DOLIN ROUGE**
- Dry vermouth: **DOLIN DRY, MARTINI & ROSSI,** or **CARPANO**
- Orange liqueur: **COINTREAU, GRAND MARNIER, DRY CURAÇAO**

- [ ] **Fresh herbs:** If you want to go the extra mile, mint, basil, and rosemary all have a place in your home bar and are great for garnishes and making flavored simple syrups (more on that on page 227).

- [ ] **Pickled veggies:** Olives, pickled okra, and other pickled vegetables can come into play for martinis and Bloody Marys. They also happen to make great snacks!

Smoky Paloma (page 222)

ESSENTIAL SPIRITS, BRANDS, AND RECIPES TO GET STARTED

Now, for the main event: the hard liquor. In the next few pages, we're going over a basic and non-exhaustive list of liquors we'd like to see in your home bar, and a little info about each. We're also sharing our house recipes for two classic cocktails per spirit: one in single-serving quantities and one in a batch format for six to eight servings, which you can prepare ahead of time when hosting small groups.

The Lemon Drop—Batch Style

Vodka

Brands we recommend: TITO'S, KETEL ONE

Vodka, the angelic taste of nothing but pure alcohol. Given that the process for making vodka involves a whole bunch of distilling to remove all the impurities, the difference in quality between lower-end stuff and high-end stuff isn't quite as obvious as in, say, tequila and whiskey. Cheap vodka isn't, like, great, but it's not going to turn your insides into the pits of hell quite as much as some other cheap liquors. We usually stick to mid-range vodka that gets the job done just fine.

The Perfect Dirty Vodka Martini

2 ounces (60 ml) **TITO'S** or other vodka

¾ ounce (22 ml) **DOLIN DRY** or other dry vermouth

¾ ounce (22 ml) olive juice

2 dashes orange bitters

1 blue cheese–stuffed olive, skewered, for garnish

Combine all the ingredients (besides the olive) in a mixing glass. Fill with ice and stir 20 to 30 times. Strain into a chilled coupe glass (because martini glasses are stupid and top-heavy), and garnish with the olive.

The Lemon Drop— Batch Style

1½ cups (360 ml) **TITO'S** or other vodka

1 cup (240 ml) **COINTREAU** or other orange liqueur

⅓ cup (75 ml) lemon juice

¼ cup (60 ml) simple syrup (recipe on page 227)

2 cups (480 ml) ice, plus more for serving

Sugar, for garnish, optional

LUXARDO cherries, for garnish, optional

Orange wedges, for garnish, optional

Combine the vodka, Cointreau, and lemon juice in a serving pitcher and mix to combine. Fill pitcher with ice and stir well—it's okay for the ice to melt, cocktails need a bit of water content! Prepare the serving glasses by rimming with sugar (wet the outer rim of the glass with the corner of a lemon wedge and roll it in a shallow dish of sugar so the granules stick) then filling with ice. Pour into individual glasses as needed and garnish each glass with a Luxardo cherry or orange wedge.

Rum

Brands we recommend: CAÑA BRAVA, FLOR DE CAÑA 4-YEAR, EL DORADO 5-YEAR, MYERS'S RUM

Rums come in a huge range of flavor profiles, from white (or "silver") rum that's clear in color and fresh tasting, "gold" rum with vanilla and caramel notes, and dark or black rum that can have notes of cola, clove, and even cherry.

Generally, the darker the rum, the deeper and richer the flavor—lighter rums are great for low-proof shaken cocktails and darker ones can make incredible Rum Old Fashioneds. Cheaply made "spiced rum" and rum-based liqueurs like Malibu have given rum a bad name, but rum can be a complex and beautiful liquor if you know what you're looking for.

Daiquiri

2 ounces (60 ml) white aged rum, such as **FLOR DE CAÑA 4-YEAR**

1 ounce (30 ml) simple syrup (see page 227)

1 ounce (30 ml) lime juice

Combine all the ingredients in a cocktail shaker. Shake for 15 to 20 seconds and strain into a coupe or rocks glass.

Hot tip: For an even more complex daiquiri with an enjoyably rich and bitter element, add ½ ounce (15 ml) amaro—**AMARO MONTENEGRO** or **CYNAR** is great.

Dark and Stormy— Batch Style

1½ cups (360 ml) white rum, such as **CAÑA BRAVA**

¾ cup (180 ml) lime juice

2 (12-ounce/360 ml) ginger beers

4 ounces (120 ml) or so dark rum (½ ounce/15 ml per serving), such as **MYERS'S RUM ORIGINAL DARK**

Candied ginger, for garnish

Combine the rum, lime juice, and ginger beer in a pitcher with ice. Stir and pour into serving glasses. Top each drink with a splash of dark rum to make it "stormy." For a cute interactive twist, try setting out the dark rum floater in a separate, smaller pitcher for your guests to DIY their stormies. Garnish the glasses with candied ginger.

Daiquiri

Manhattan

Whiskey

Brands we recommend for Bourbon:
FOUR ROSES, WILD TURKEY; **and for rye:**
RITTENHOUSE

Whiskey's flavor profile can range from sweet and caramelly to spicy, floral, smoky, or even briny. Bourbon is the people-pleaser among American whiskeys, typically having an easy-drinking vanilla flavor profile and soft texture. Rye has more of a spicy and grainy bite, making it great for those who like something less sweet. We're sticking to these two styles here, but some other popular categories of whiskey are Scotch, Canadian, Japanese, Irish, and Tennessee whiskey—dive into some of those if you really want to round out your whiskey knowledge!

Manhattan

2 ounces (60 ml) **RITTENHOUSE RYE** or whiskey of your choice

1 ounce (30 ml) **COCCHI VERMOUTH DI TORINO** or sweet vermouth of your choice

2 dashes **REGAN'S ORANGE BITTERS**

Luxardo cherry or orange peel, for garnish

Combine the rye, sweet vermouth, and orange bitters in a mixing glass over ice and stir for 20 rotations. Strain into a chilled coupe glass. Garnish as desired.

Whiskey Smash— Batch Style

1 cup (240 ml) **FOUR ROSES BOURBON**

¾ cup (180 ml) lemon juice

½ cup (120 ml) mint simple syrup (recipe below)

1 cup (240 ml) ice cubes, plus crushed ice for serving

Club soda, to top off each serving

Mint sprigs, for garnish

Combine the bourbon, lemon juice, and mint simple syrup in a pitcher or serving container. Add ice and stir. Fill the serving glasses with crushed ice, then pour the cocktail until the glasses are three-quarters full. Top each serving with club soda and a sprig of mint.

Mint Simple Syrup

Makes 1 cup (240 ml)

1 cup (200 g) sugar

½ cup (5 g) fresh mint leaves

In a saucepan, bring ½ cup (120 ml) water to a boil. Add the sugar and stir until completely dissolved. Remove from heat and pour the syrup over the mint leaves in a small bowl. Steep for 20 minutes, then strain and discard the mint leaves. Let cool before using or storing in an airtight container, refrigerated, for up to 1 month.

Tequila and Mezcal

Brand we recommend for mezcal:
DEL MAGUEY VIDA; **and for tequila:**
CASAMIGOS, ESPOLÓN

Tequila and mezcal are both made from the agave plant, but they can taste totally different from each other. Tequila tends to have a brighter, cleaner flavor than mezcal, which is usually rich and often smoky. Quality tequila and mezcal are fantastic sipped on their own, but also work beautifully in cocktail recipes.

Smoky Paloma

2 ounces (60 ml) **DEL MAGUEY VIDA** mezcal

3 ounces (90 ml) grapefruit juice

¾ ounce (22 ml) agave nectar

¼ teaspoon sea salt

About 2 ounces (60ml) club soda

Rosemary sprig, for garnish

Add all the ingredients except the soda to a cocktail shaker with ice and shake vigorously for 15 to 20 seconds. Pour into a Collins or other tall glass, top with soda, and garnish with rosemary.

Pitcher o' Margs

2 cups (480 ml) **ESPOLÓN REPOSADO**

1 cup (240 ml) **COINTREAU** or other orange liqueur

¾ cup (180 ml) lime juice

3 cups (720 ml) ice

Sea salt, for garnish

Combine all the ingredients in a pitcher and stir to evenly mix. Serve by pouring into glasses rimmed with coarse sea salt, if desired. To rim a glass, wet the outer edge by rubbing it with the corner of a lime wedge and roll it in a shallow dish of salt so the salt sticks.

Pitcher o' Margs

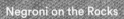

Negroni on the Rocks

Gin

Brands we recommend: BEEFEATER, HAYMAN'S OLD TOM

Gin is a clear liquor that typically leans aromatic and herbaceous. The most popular style of gin is London Dry Gin, which has subtle notes of pine, citrus peel, and juniper, but some gins will lean extremely floral, almost smelling like a citrusy bouquet of flowers, or incredibly aromatic in a way that's more like a perfume.

Negroni

1 ounce (30 ml) **BEEFEATER** gin

1 ounce (30 ml) **COCCHI VERMOUTH DI TORINO** or sweet vermouth of your choice

1 ounce (30 ml) **CAMPARI**

Orange twist, for garnish

Combine all the ingredients in a mixing glass and add ice. Stir, then strain over fresh ice in a rocks glass, or serve up in a chilled coupe glass. Garnish with the orange twist.

Tom Collins—Batch Style

1½ cups (360 ml) **HAYMAN'S OLD TOM** gin

¾ cup (180 ml) lemon juice

¾ cup (180 ml) simple syrup (see page 227)

2 cups (480 ml) ice

Chilled sparkling water, to top each drink (or sparkling wine to make it a French 75!)

Orange wheels, for garnish

Add the gin, lemon juice, simple syrup, and ice to a pitcher. Stir to combine thoroughly. Serve by filling glasses about three-quarters full, then top with sparkling water, or sparkling wine if preferred. Garnish with an orange wheel.

WHEN TO SHAKE? WHEN TO STIR?

To put it simply, you should shake anything that has citrus juice, cream, or egg.* The ice getting jostled around with those ingredients will improve the texture of the drink, giving you a beautifully velvety and frothy cocktail. Stir basically everything else. James Bond (and a bunch of copycats after him) ordered shaken martinis but that's technically "wrong." If that's how you like it, please carry on, but we're just giving you all the info, okay?!

* We don't get into it much in this chapter, but yes, cream and even raw egg are both commonly found ingredients in cocktails! These cocktails get DRY SHAKEN (shaken before adding ice) in order to properly whip the cream or egg, and then shaken a second time with ice. Try out a Ramos Gin Fizz or Whiskey Flip to get started using them.

Developing Original Cocktails: Templates and Ratios

For anyone who watched the 1-800-BARTEND commercials in the early 2000s and felt a glimmer of hope for the first time, this one's for you! It's super easy to start developing your own seasonal or original twists and make your friends and loved ones wonder when you had the time to become a master of booze. Your father-in-law will see you in action and call you a mixologist, and you'll cringe at the use of that word, but deep inside, it'll feel good.

Sticking to the template of classic cocktails gives you a road map for developing your own creations. For simplicity's sake, we're breaking down types of cocktails into three main templates that are easy to riff off of—old fashioneds, sours, and booze-on-booze—and giving some thought starters for how to plug in your own ideas

HOW TO MAKE SIMPLE SYRUP AND FLAVORED SIMPLE SYRUPS

For plain ol' simple syrup, bring one part water to a boil over medium heat. Add two parts granulated sugar to the water and stir until the sugar has dissolved completely. Remove from heat and cool to room temperature before using or storing in an airtight container. Store for up to 1 month in the fridge.

You can also create flavored simple syrups to jumpstart your original cocktail ideas or to use with club soda or tonic for simple "mocktails." There are a few easy ways to do this.

- Replace the water with an already flavored liquid such as Earl Grey, agua de Jamaica (hibiscus tea), coconut water, coffee, or green tea.

- For herb-infused simple syrups, boil sugar and water together as in the instructions above, and when all the sugar has dissolved, add fresh herbs and boil for 1 more minute.

Remove from heat and allow to steep for 30 minutes. Pass through a fine-mesh strainer to remove the solids before using or storing.

- For syrups flavored with extracts (almond, vanilla, orange, etc.), make your simple syrup and allow it to fully cool before adding 1 to 1½ teaspoons extract, to taste, per 1 cup (240 ml) simple syrup and stir to fully incorporate.

- For fruit syrups, bring 1 part fresh or frozen fruit, 1 part sugar, and ½ part water to a boil in a saucepan, then reduce to a simmer. Mash the fruit as it cooks. When you have a thick syrupy consistency, remove from heat and pass through a fine-mesh strainer to remove the solids. Thin this syrup to your preference by adding more water, and reserve the solids to put on top of toast or pancakes.

Old-Fashioned Cocktails

Our Old-Fashioned recipe—pretty close to what you'll get if you order an Old-Fashioned at any bar—is super straightforward: 2 ounces (60 ml) bourbon or rye, ½ ounce (15 ml) simple syrup, and 2 dashes angostura bitters stirred over ice in a mixing glass and garnished with an orange twist. But you can make an "old-fashioned" cocktail with any spirit. There are already many popular drinks that are slight alterations like the Sazerac, the Oaxacan Old-Fashioned, and countless "house special" cocktails that you've probably ordered at a hip new bar run by the demure, skinny guy with the apron and the neck tattoo.

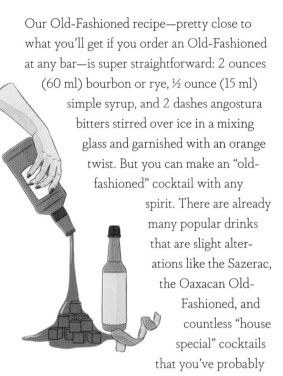

Changing out the base spirit is just the starting point. If you want to further push your creativity you can use flavored simple syrups: think along the lines of a basil-infused simple syrup with rum or strawberry simple syrup with a tequila base. As for the bitters, there are literally thousands of options—each one able to bring a totally different flavor profile to your drink.

Rum Old-Fashioned

Makes 1 drink

2 ounces (60 ml) 3- to 5-year aged rum, such as EL DORADO 5-YEAR

¾ ounce (22 ml) vanilla simple syrup (see page 227 for making flavored simple syrups)

2 dashes coffee bitters

Orange peel, for garnish

Stir the rum, simple syrup, and bitters together in a mixing glass over ice for about 20 rotations before straining into an old-fashioned glass filled with fresh ice and garnishing with an orange peel.

Sours

The sour category of cocktail is pretty easy to spot: Basically, does it have citrus juice? If so, it's a sour. A common drink in this category is, of course, the whiskey sour. But also grouped here are the margarita, daiquiri, sidecar, French 75, and many more. These should always be shaken, not stirred, as the ice interacting with the fruit juice creates a lovely texture and brightness.

This template has some room for improvisation, but in its purest form consists of three ingredients in a 2:1:1 ratio of spirit : citrus : syrup (or sweet liqueur). Sours that use sweet

liqueur instead of syrup can be, you know, dangerous, because they're pretty alcohol-heavy but with a light and bright taste that makes them go down easy. Before you know

it you're "causing trouble" and "being asked to leave," or, to share a personal anecdote of ours, looking your new boyfriend dead in the eye and saying, "Do you want a big scene or a little scene, because right now it's little, but it can get real big real quick." We were an instant match. So anyway, use this template to create your own refreshing sippers, or check out our Cherry-Lime Gin Cocktail!

Cherry–Lime Gin Cocktail

Makes 1 drink

2 ounces (60 ml) BEEFEATER gin

1 ounce (30 ml) CHERRY HEERING

¾ ounce (22 ml) lime juice

¼ ounce (7 ml) COCCHI VERMOUTH DI TORINO, or other sweet vermouth

Luxardo cherry, for garnish

Combine the gin, cherry liqueur, lime juice, and vermouth in a cocktail shaker with ice and shake. Strain and serve up in a coupe glass. Garnish with a Luxardo cherry.

Booze-on-Booze Cocktails

These are your Manhattans, your Negronis, and your classic martinis—the category where all of the ingredients contain some amount of alcohol. No citrus juices and no separate sugar or simple syrup. They should always be stirred and not shaken. This type of cocktail is probably the toughest to riff on (sorry!) because you have to be pretty familiar with your liquors and liqueurs to make compelling and delicious combinations.

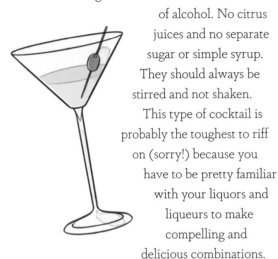

The thing about spirits and liqueurs is that two different products, such as two brands of sweet vermouth, could yield a completely different-tasting drink. The key is to continually taste and familiarize yourself with your ingredients, noting what you like and don't like about each one.

The basic ratio for this category is 2:1 (two parts base liquor to one part aperitif or liqueur), but commonly that can look like 1:1:1 (one part base liquor to one part each of two different aperitifis or liqueurs), and again there's plenty of room to adjust. Basically, you're taking a stronger spirit and cutting that with a lower ABV (that's alcohol by volume) aperitif or liqueur.

Negroni Rosa

Makes 1 drink

1 ounce (30 ml) HAYMAN'S OLD TOM gin

1 ounce (30 ml) DOLIN BLANC vermouth

1 ounce (30 ml) APEROL

Grapefruit twist, for garnish

Combine the gin, vermouth, and Aperol in a mixing glass with ice and stir for 20 to 30 rotations. Strain over ice in an old-fashioned glass (or serve up in a coupe glass) and garnish with a grapefruit twist.

FEEL IT, PEEL IT, SQUEEZE IT, RUB IT

For citrus peel garnishes, use a citrus peeler to get the best strip of rind possible. You can feel how good a citrus fruit is for garnish by touch—the thicker the skin the better it is for garnish (and the thinner it is, the better it is for juicing . . . go figure). Peel the rind off then squeeze it over itself near the drink to express the faintest hint of citrus oil. Then rub the outside of the peel all around the rim of the glass and fold and rest it on the rim, or just plop it right in.

CHAPTER 23

Favorites from Our Kitchen

Okay, so we've gotten all the drinks taken care of, and now it's time to focus on feeding the hungry masses. We love challenging ourselves in the kitchen, but when we're having people over we tend to stick to tried-and-true comfort-food favorites that cut back on dishes and are easy to serve family-style. We're sharing a few of the dishes that we make the most and never get tired of. Try 'em out next time you're having friends come by.

One of the first things we bonded over back when we first met was our mutual love of being in the kitchen. So cliché, but true! To this day it's the most used space in our home, and it's where we have our best conversations, biggest arguments, and come up with our favorite recipes. When we have folks over, the kitchen is a natural gathering spot, and it's not uncommon for friends to join in on

helping us prepare a meal. Enjoying a meal together is one of our favorite ways to bond with our guests, but making that meal together can be even more rewarding. Don't be afraid to let your guests jump in and lend a helping hand.

Party Favor Pepper Jelly

Many many years ago, we randomly ended up with a gigantically enormous sack of about-to-go-bad bell peppers in our local CSA delivery. After frantically making fajitas several nights in a row, we realized we had to use them all immediately, so we decided to learn how to make a childhood favorite: pepper jelly, a sweet and spicy jelly that can be paired with cream cheese and crackers, served on biscuits for breakfast, or whisked with a little vinegar, oil, and Dijon mustard to make a vinaigrette. After a little bit of research we improvised a recipe, spicing things up by doing a 50/50 split of bell peppers and jalapeños. We wound up with more pepper jelly than any normal household should contain, so it became a party favor—a handout of little jars to our friends as they left our home. We saved the recipe and worked on it in the years following, usually in the fall and winter, and would sometimes deliver jars with a note to our people for the holidays.

We specify that you use Pamona's pectin, as it gives a jellied consistency even with the relatively low sugar content. Other pectins may require a much higher amount of sugar to properly gel, though you can experiment with other low-sugar pectins if you'd like!

Takes 1 hour
Makes 12 half pints (1.4 liters)

1 (1¾ oz) pack Pomona's pectin (includes calcium packet)

7 cups sugar

12 half-pint canning jars (480 ml each) with two-piece sealing lids

2 pounds (910 g) green bell peppers

2 pounds (910 g) jalapeño chiles

1½ cups (354 ml) apple cider vinegar

2 orange, yellow, or red bell peppers (or a mix!), seeded and roughly chopped

1 Combine ¼ teaspoon of the calcium included in your Pomona's pectin with ¼ cup water in a lidded jar and shake to combine. Set aside. In a separate bowl, whisk together the pectin with the sugar and set aside.

2 Sterilize your jars and lids by boiling them in a large pot of water for 10 minutes. Water should cover the jars by at least 1 inch (2.5 cm). Use tongs to remove and set aside. You may need to do this in two batches, depending on the size of your pot. You'll want the jars to still be warm when it's time to fill them in step 5, so don't do this step ahead of time. Instead, do it just before or concurrently with the following steps.

3 Remove the stems and seeds of the green bell peppers and jalapeños and give them a rough chop. Puree them together with the vinegar to break the peppers down into a thick puree with some remaining chunks. If using an immersion blender, the easy way to do this is to add the peppers to the pot you plan to cook the jelly in and blend it all in there (and then you're ready to start step 4!). Otherwise, blending them in a food processor or blender works fine.

4 Combine the puree, chopped bell peppers, and ¼ cup calcium water in a large pot and bring to a rolling boil (a hard, continuous boil that doesn't stop when you give it a good stirring). Boil for 2 minutes, stirring constantly. Add the pectin/sugar mix and stir to dissolve. Return to a hard boil and boil for 2 minutes, stirring constantly. Remove from the heat.

5 Immediately ladle the mixture into the jars, leaving ¼ inch of room at the top. Wipe clean any spills on the rim of each jar and tightly seal with the two-piece lids.

6 Use your tongs to gently lower the jars right side up into a pot of boiling water (the water must entirely cover the jars by at least 1 inch [2.5 cm]) and boil them for 10 minutes. Gently remove each jar from the pot using the tongs and set, right side up, on a towel to cool undisturbed. Don't tilt or shake the jars during this time, as it may interrupt the sealing process. After the jars have cooled completely, let them sit at room temperature for another 24 hours. Within the first few hours, the jars should seal and will often make a loud clicking noise as they do so (see Note). Sealed jars can be stored for up to a year in a cool, dry, dark place.

NOTE: To test the seal, press down on the top of the lid. If the top can be pressed down, it hasn't sealed yet. If you have any jars that are unsealed after 24 hours, you can remove the jelly from those jars and reheat it just to boiling, then re-sterilize the jars and repeat the sealing process. Alternatively, just refrigerate any unsealed jars and commit to using them within two weeks.

Kale Caesar

We can hear you groaning—Caesar salad? How basic-Italian-restaurant-from-1998 can you get? Okay well first off, what on earth did we do to you??? This salad is one of our favorite recipes to make and share, and it's probably our most popular recipe in terms of how often other people make it—friends, family, and folks who follow our blog. Big important things: Don't skip cracking the black pepper fresh, don't skimp on the anchovy or omit the egg yolk, and use the highest-quality olive oil and Parmesan you can find.

Takes 10 minutes
Makes 4 servings

4 cloves garlic, peeled

Pinch quality salt and fresh cracked black pepper

3 whole anchovy fillets or 1½ teaspoons anchovy paste

1 egg yolk

1 tablespoon Dijon mustard

Juice of 1 lemon

⅓ cup (30 g) finely grated Parmesan

About ⅓ cup (75 ml) olive oil (or more for desired consistency)

1 large bunch kale, chopped to desired size (you'll need about 8 ounces [225 g] leaves; see Notes)

½ cup (50 g) Parmesan shavings

Croutons, preferably home-made (optional; see Notes)

1 Add the garlic, salt, and pepper to a large wooden bowl and use a muddler or pestle to pound the garlic until a paste forms with only a few small remaining chunks. Add the anchovies and muddle them into the garlic.

2 Whisk in the egg yolk, followed by the mustard and lemon juice. Whisk just to combine.

3 Slowly whisk in the grated Parmesan to form a paste.

4 Finally, drizzle in the olive oil, whisking the entire time. If you want a thinner dressing, add extra oil, a tablespoon at a time, until your desired consistency is reached.

5 Use tongs to toss half the kale into the dressing until fully coated. Add the remaining kale and toss again. Top with the Parmesan shavings and croutons (if using) and enjoy!

NOTES: Baby kale will provide a milder texture and flavor and can be used whole, lacinato kale will be rather rough and earthy and is best chopped more finely, and curly kale falls between the two in both flavor and texture and will need just a rough chop.

To make croutons, we cube half a baguette, toss it in enough olive oil to thoroughly coat it, sprinkle on salt, and bake in a preheated 375°F (190°C) oven for 8 to 10 minutes, flipping each piece over halfway through.

YOUR VINAIGRETTE TEMPLATE

Between all the unnecessary packaging and potential for sketchy ingredients, store-bought salad dressings are kind of a scam, honestly. Use our dressing template and plug in whatever ingredients you have on hand, letting your intuition and occasional pinky dips, to taste, guide you.

2 PARTS OIL + 1 PART ACID + EMULSIFYING AGENT + "OTHER STUFF"

2 parts oil: Extra-virgin olive oil, grapeseed oil, avocado oil, canola oil, and even walnut or sesame oil work well here. You can use a totally neutral oil like canola if you're letting the other ingredients take center stage, or something with more flavor like walnut oil, or a combination of oils, like a small amount of robust toasted sesame oil toned down by a neutral grapeseed oil.

1 part acid: We're talking vinegar and/or fresh citrus juice. Lemon juice and apple cider vinegar are what we usually reach for, but if we want to add a touch of sweetness, we'll use orange juice, or if we're aiming for, say, a Southeast Asian flavor profile, lime juice can work well. Quality balsamic vinegar can pack a punch of flavor on its own, but if you want the acidity to be more neutral to highlight other flavors in your dressing, something like champagne vinegar or white wine vinegar does the trick. Red wine vinegar is another staple in our on-the-fly salad dressings for a simple vinaigrette made with olive oil, salt, pepper, and Dijon mustard.

Emulsifying agent: An emulsifier is essential to make sure the oil and vinegar don't separate, which is basically just a really sad tragic thing to happen on a salad. You'll want to use at least a tablespoon per cup of dressing. Our standby recommendation for this is just Dijon mustard, but you can also use some storebought or homemade mayonnaise for an emulsifier with a little less bite, a single egg yolk for a creamy textured dressing like the one used in our Kale Caesar (page 236), or even tomato paste (really!) if the flavor makes sense with the other ingredients you're using, like in a tomato balsamic vinaigrette.

Other stuff: The oil, acid, and emulsifying agents are the foundation of your dressing, but this is your opportunity to pack in the flavor. Fresh herbs like dill, mint, or basil; sweeteners like honey or jam; grated or crumbled cheeses like Parmesan, feta, or Cotija; minced shallot or garlic or fresh ginger that's been ground with a pestle; creamy nut and seed butters like tahini, sunflower butter, or peanut butter; nuts like pepitas and almonds; and other flavorful ingredients like soy sauce and chili paste.

Whisk everything together in your serving bowl in the order listed above, add your greens, give it a gentle toss, and serve immediately.

Red Beans and Rice

A New Orleans classic that we love to make ahead of any party calling for a Big Pot of Something, this Red Beans and Rice recipe is a staple in our home. It's traditionally made for Monday-night dinner, but no day is better to enjoy a bowl than the day or two after you make it—this is one of those "gets better in the fridge" situations. Our recipe utilizes apple cider vinegar to punch up the acidity without overdoing the heat. There's still plenty of spice from the hot sauce, but that vinegar trick gives the other aromatic flavors a chance to shine through, too. Our serving recommendation is to top a bowl of these beans with a heap of white rice, a few dashes of Crystal hot sauce, and the fluffiest, butteriest cornbread you can manage to get or prepare. We proudly and unironically stick to a box of Jiffy.

Takes 10 hours in a slow-cooker
Makes 8 to 10 servings

2 tablespoons unsalted butter

14 ounces (400 g) smoked sausages, sliced into ¼-inch rounds

4 large stalks celery, finely chopped

1 yellow onion, chopped

1 green bell pepper, chopped

⅓ cup (17 g) chopped fresh parsley, slightly packed, plus extra for garnish

3 large cloves garlic, minced

1 pound (454 g) dry kidney beans

2 bay leaves

6 cups (1.4 liters) chicken stock (see Notes)

¼ cup (60 ml) apple cider vinegar

¼ cup (60 ml) hot sauce (we always use Crystal brand), or more to taste

2 boullion cubes, optional (to add flavor)

Fresh cracked pepper, salt, and crushed red pepper

Fresh-cooked white rice and corn bread, for serving

Continues

1 In a cast-iron skillet or frying pan, melt the butter over medium-high heat. Add the sausage rounds and brown them, about 2 to 3 minutes on each side.

2 Transfer the sausage and drippings into a slow cooker, along with literally all of the remaining ingredients (other than the rice and cornbread). Give a good stir and set to the low setting. Let simmer, covered, for 10 hours (see Notes). In the last hour, use a potato smasher to smash about half of the beans into a creamy consistency, give a good stir, and let them finish cooking. Taste and season with any additional salt, pepper, or crushed red pepper you may desire.

3 Serve with fresh-cooked white rice and corn bread. Garnish with parsley. Leftovers will last in an airtight container in the refrigerator for up to 1 week.

NOTES: The longer you let them sit in the slow cooker, the thicker, creamier, and more amorphous the beans will be. Keep the cook time shorter if you want the dish soupier and the beans more whole and separate.

You can get creative with the stock. We once found a good deal on a whole rabbit, and after we enjoyed that, we made some stock that found its way into our red beans the next week. Red beans traditionalists will tell you to add a bone-in ham hock, which flavors the liquid as the beans cook, much like stock. Use what you have on hand and opt for flavorful homemade stock whenever possible—it makes a huge difference.

Pasta Bolognese

We were both raised in Italian-American families where "red gravy" and "meat sauce" were nothing short of staples, especially for larger family gatherings, whether it was a reunion, a holiday, a birthday, or just your occasional big family dinner when Cousin Tony got out of jail. We've kept that tradition up in our home and love to make our Bolognese whenever we've got people over for dinner or out of town visitors for the weekend. The recipe is uncomplicated but does require you to be pretty attached to your stove for about an hour, so make sure to have a glass of Chianti nearby—and if you really want to channel an Italian grandma, you've got to sip it while looking really disappointed in everyone around you.

Takes about 1½ hours
Makes 6 servings

8 ounces (225 g) dry tagliatelle or other pasta of your choice

Salt

2 tablespoons butter

1 tablespoon olive oil

4 cloves garlic, minced

1 medium onion, chopped

1 medium carrot, finely chopped

2 stalks celery, chopped

8 ounces (225 g) loose pork breakfast sausage

1 pound (455 g) lean ground beef

½ cup (120 ml) heavy cream

½ cup (120 ml) dry vermouth

1 (28-ounce/795 g) can diced tomatoes

¼ cup (13 g) chopped fresh parsley, plus more for garnish

Parmesan shavings

Fresh cracked black pepper

Continues

1   Cook the tagliatelle in salted water according to the package instructions, drain, and set aside, reserving the cooking water.

2   In a large pot, heat the butter and olive oil until the butter begins to bubble. Add the garlic, onion, and a pinch of salt and cook over medium-high heat until the onions are translucent, about 8 to 10 minutes, stirring often to avoid browning. Add the carrot and celery and sauté an additional 5 minutes.

3   Add the pork and beef, breaking the ground meat apart with your spoon, and incorporate it well into vegetables. Cook until the meat is browned, about 5 minutes.

4   Add the cream and ½ cup (120 ml) of the reserved pasta water. Stir frequently until the liquid has bubbled off, about 8 minutes. Add the vermouth and another ½ cup pasta (120 ml) water and, like above, stir frequently until the liquid has bubbled off, about 8 minutes. Add the diced tomatoes and stir to incorporate thoroughly. Add the parsley and stir to combine.

5   Lower the heat to a simmer and cook the sauce, covered, for about 1 hour. During this time, season with salt and pepper to taste.

6   Add the prepared pasta to the pot of sauce and stir to heat and combine. Serve with fresh parsley and shaved Parmesan.

Blueberry Earl Grey Scones with Earl Grey Glaze

We personally love low expectations, and in the world of baked goods, scones are about as low as you can get—they can often be dry, lack flavor, and make you hate yourself for ever deciding to eat one in the first place. Not these! These babies are moist and cakey and filled with juicy blueberries and bright citrus flavors and floral notes from the Earl Grey that will delight your friends' and family's taste buds. They're one of our favorite things to serve at a brunch or other daytime event and are the perfect complement to a few mimosas. We first shared these on our blog many years ago and they quickly became a hit, so we hope you'll give this easy recipe a try.

Takes 1 hour
Makes 8 scones

2 cups plus 1 tablespoon (297 g) all-purpose flour

⅓ cup (65 g) sugar

2½ teaspoons baking powder

½ teaspoon ground cinnamon

1 teaspoon finely ground Earl Grey tea

1 teaspoon kosher salt

½ cup (1 stick; 115 g) very cold unsalted butter (you can pop it in the freezer for 30 minutes before using)

½ cup (120 ml) whole milk

1 large egg

1 teaspoon vanilla extract

Zest of 1 orange

1 cup (145 g) frozen blueberries

FOR THE GLAZE

1 cup (100 g) confectioners' sugar

2 teaspoons finely ground Earl Grey tea

1 tablespoon whole milk

¼ teaspoon vanilla extract

¼ teaspoon orange extract

Continues

1 With a rack in the center position, preheat the oven to 400°F (200°C). Line a baking sheet with parchment paper and set aside.

2 Use a wire whisk to whisk together the flour, sugar, baking powder, cinnamon, ground tea, and salt in a large bowl. Use the large shredding side of a box grater to grate the butter over the flour mixture, folding in the butter as you go. Then, use your whisk like a potato masher (pounding it up and down into the flour) to cut in the butter until there are no butter lumps larger than a pea.

3 In a small bowl, whisk together the milk, egg, vanilla extract, and orange zest and pour it evenly over the flour mixture, using a rubber spatula or spoon to mix in evenly without overworking the batter—it should be crumbly. Fold in the blueberries, being careful not to break them apart (though, if they're totally frozen this shouldn't be a problem).

4 Flour your hands and transfer all the dough directly onto the prepared baking sheet and form it into a disk, roughly 8 inches (20 cm) across and 1 inch (2.5 cm) thick. Use a sharp knife to cut it into 8 slices like you'd cut a pizza, and use an offset spatula or pie knife to gently pull the slices about 4 inches (10 cm) apart from each other to give the scones room to rise.

5 Bake for 20 to 25 minutes until golden brown on top. Remove from the oven and let cool on a wire rack.

6 Meanwhile, make the glaze: Whisk together all ingredients in a bowl until the confectioners' sugar is dissolved. Once the scones have cooled, drizzle or spoon the glaze over the tops and enjoy.

THAT'S THE END!

Thank you for joining us on this book journey. We didn't put blood, sweat, or tears into it (sick! why would you want that!), but we did spend a lot of very early mornings and late nights trying to make this book as clear and perfect for you as we could. We racked our brains on what absolutely needed to be included and what absolutely shouldn't be, fought over which conjunctions belonged where, and forced our friends to help do things like hold up the little light diffuser thingies for photo shoots and read extremely rough drafts of various chapters we struggled with. Whether you're already seasoned in any of the topics we've covered, or totally new to the realms of homemaking, we hope this book has given you the confidence, tools, and inspiration you need to create a home life that is perfect for you and all of the loved ones you share it with.

Acknowledgments

As much as we would love to take all the credit for this book, there are so many people whom we relied on to make it happen.

Thanks to our friend Lily Diamond for giving us the pep talk we needed to believe we (us!) could write a book in the first place, and for connecting us with our incredible agent, Nicole Tourtelot. And thank you to Nicole for believing in our ideas for this book and working so hard to find the right publisher for it.

Thanks to Laura Dozier, Danielle Youngsmith, and the entire team at Abrams for trusting our vision and holding our hands through this whole process; we would've been completely lost without their guidance.

Thanks so much to our incredibly talented photographer, Augusta Sagnelli, for the beautiful images she contributed, and to our bestie and assistant stylist Morgan Hanson for assisting us with the most chaotic photoshoot schedule we could've planned. Also sorry.

To our illustrator, Stephanie Singleton, for so quickly embracing this project and understanding what we wanted to achieve by including her illustrations; we are so grateful. It wouldn't be the same book without her work!

Thank you so much to our best friends for lending us your homes and/or furniture for photo shoots, and for constantly hyping us up and reading very rough sections to see if it was going to be any good. Hayli, Camille, Matt W., Allison, Morgan, Chris, Thomas, and PJ: we love you! And to our moms, Janie and Perri, who would never let us hear the end of it if we didn't include them on this page—we love you dearly.

Thank you to our tiny best friend, Fox, for sitting so still and being a very good boy while we spent hours glued to our computers.

And finally, thanks *so very much* to everybody who reads our blog and newsletter or follows our lives and work on social media. Without your support this book literally never could have been a possibility.

Further Reading

In case we've piqued your interest in any of the topics we've touched on, we've listed a few of our favorite books below. These are books we find ourselves constantly turning to for inspiration and information, and we think you'll love them, too.

Designing and Decorating

Vintage Living: Creating a Beautiful Home with Treasured Objects from the Past by Bob Richter

Home for the Soul: Sustainable and Thoughtful Decorating and Design by Sara Bird

Modern Mix: Curating Personal Style with Chic & Accessible Finds by Eddie Ross

The New Bohemians Handbook: Come Home to Good Vibes by Justina Blakeney

Styled: Secrets for Arranging Rooms, from Tabletops to Bookshelves by Emily Henderson

Living with Color: Inspiration and How-Tos to Brighten Up Your Home by Rebecca Atwood

DIY and Plant Care

Vintage Home: Stylish Ideas and over 50 Handmade Projects from Furniture to Decorating by Sarah Moore

Beginner's Guide to DIY & Home Repair: Essential DIY Techniques for the First Timer by Jo Behari and Alison Winfield-Chislett

Wild at Home: How to Style and Care for Beautiful Plants by Hilton Carter

Container Gardening for Beginners: A Guide to Growing Your Own Vegetables, Fruits, Herbs, and Edible Flowers by Tammy Wylie

The Martha Manual: How to Do (Almost) Everything by Martha Stewart

Entertaining, Food, and Drink

The Gift of Gathering: Beautiful Tablescapes to Welcome & Celebrate Your Friends and Family by Bre Doucette

The Modern Bohemian Table: Gathering with Friends & Entertaining in Style by Amanda Bernardi

That Cheese Plate Will Change Your Life: Creative Gatherings and Self-Care with the Cheese by Numbers Method by Marissa Mullen

Wine Simple: A Totally Approachable Guide from a World-Class Sommelier by Aldo Sohm

The Wine Bible by Karen MacNeil

Wine Folly: Magnum Edition: The Master Guide by Madeline Puckette and Justin Hammack

Death & Co.: Modern Classic Cocktails by David Kaplan and Nick Fauchald

Tiki: Modern Tropical Cocktails by Shannon Mustipher

Good Drinks: Alcohol-Free Recipes for When You're Not Drinking for Whatever Reason by Julia Bainbridge

The Year of Cozy: 125 Recipes, Crafts, and Other Homemade Adventures by Adrianna Adarme

Index

Note: Page numbers in *italics* indicate recipes.

Editor: Laura Dozier
Designer: Danielle Youngsmith
Managing Editor: Lisa Silverman
Production Manager: Denise LaCongo

Library of Congress Control Number: 2021946836

ISBN: 978-1-4197-5483-8
eISBN: 978-1-64700-302-9

Text copyright © 2022 Beau Ciolino and Matt Armato
Photographs copyright © Beau Ciolino and Matt Armato, except pp. 3–4,
8, 18, 20, 22, 26, 36, 38–39, 44–45, 49, 58–59, 67, 72, 74, 75 (top), 76–77,
87, 92, 94, 95 (top), 97, 110, 124, 129, 133, 164, 168, 171–72, 175–76, 178,
210, 247 copyright © Augusta Sagnelli; p. 109 copyright © Dabito
Illustrations copyright © Stephanie Singleton
Renderings: pp. 31, 34, 114 copyright © Beau Ciolino and Matt Armato;
p. 33 copyright © Jillian Mann

Cover © 2022 Abrams

Published in 2022 by Abrams, an imprint of ABRAMS. All rights reserved.
No portion of this book may be reproduced, stored in a retrieval system, or
transmitted in any form or by any means, mechanical, electronic, photocopying,
recording, or otherwise, without written permission from the publisher.

Printed and bound in the United States
10 9 8 7 6 5 4 3 2 1

The author and publisher do not accept liability for any injury, loss, or inciden-
tal or consequential damages suffered or incurred by any reader of this book.

Abrams books are available at special discounts when purchased in quantity
for premiums and promotions as well as fundraising or educational use.
Special editions can also be created to specification. For details, contact
specialsales@abramsbooks.com or the address below.

Abrams® is a registered trademark of Harry N. Abrams, Inc.

ABRAMS The Art of Books
195 Broadway, New York, NY 10007
abramsbooks.com